Joseph E. Robinson

MW01102354

Acknowledgements

No book is written alone. I would like to convey my greatest gratitude to the many people who have helped during the creation of this book – the people who: provided support, let me talk things through, read, typed, offered comments, and assisted in the editing, proofreading and design.

I would like to thank my daughter Diane for helping me to publish this book; my brother Raymond for all his input, typing, editing and patience; my grandson Rickie for his comments and for the creation of the cover page; and above all I want to thank my wife, Jeanette and the rest of my family, who supported and encouraged me. It has been an interesting and long journey to complete Japan's Honor.

Joseph E. Robinson

To Linda Oct. 4. 2015

[signature]

Chapter 1

Grandfather Kobiyashi, a widower, spends many hours and time with his only grandson, Ito. They have an extremely close relationship with each other. And like many loving grandmothers and grandfathers the world over, his grandchildren's love gave him much happiness and a will to live.

In this Japanese home, lived Ito, his mother Setsuko, and his father Sabaru Kobiyashi. Sabaru travels the world as a sales representative for a Japanese corporation and is usually away from home.

Ito loves his grandfather, and the grandfather idolizes the boy. When possible he takes Ito shopping, on trips, and to fun places.

Grandfather knows Ito's health is poor and therefore has few friends so he visits Ito's home quite often. He also relishes Ito's mother's cooking and thus endeavors to make his visits coincide

with meal times. Ito, being out of school due to summer holidays, looks forward to his grandfather's visits.

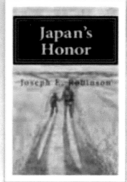

"Ito," his mother called, "Guess who is here?" The boy excitedly ran to greet his grandfather. "Grandfather it's you! I knew it would be you."

Grandfather embraced the boy. Smiling he says, "How did you know it was me?"

Ito looked up with a shy grin and replied, "Grandfather, I knew it was you because who could it be as I do not have many friends." Stepping back he poked his finger at his grandfather and said teasingly, "Whenever we have a visitor and its meal time it seems it's always you."

The grandfather laughingly said, "Well, if you must know, the truth is that it's not you but your mother's cooking that draws me here."

Ito, in a jovial manner, patted his grandfather's stomach and said, "Oh grandfather, you always say that. But you are not fooling me. I know that it's me you love the most."

Suddenly Ito's mother, bringing in refreshments, interrupts them and suggests they relax in the sitting room until the evening meal is ready.

As they sat quietly together the grandfather notices that Ito's demeanor changed. "Why all of a sudden this serious sullen face?" he asked with concern.

His head bowed and looking down to the floor, Ito was not quite sure how to respond. He quietly and slowly answered, "Grandfather, there are certain things that cause my mind and heart to be in much sadness."

His grandfather, looking worried, asked, "How can I mend this sadness?"

Reluctantly Ito responded, "Grandfather, if I tell you what troubles me will you promise that you won't be upset with me and that you will always respect my inner feelings by keeping it to yourself?"

His grandfather walked towards him, put his hands on Ito's shoulders and comfortingly said, "You must know how much love I have for you, and that no matter what you tell me I will understand and keep it to myself. So, please, speak what is on your mind."

Eyes still facing down, Ito was now feeling somewhat troubled and uncomfortable with what he had to say. "It won't be easy for me to explain exactly what I really want to say."

He lifted his head, and looking directly into his grandfather's eyes, and with much nervousness, stammered, "Well, as you know my ambition someday is to be a famous writer. I am highly recognized in school for my written poems and short stories. So in my desire to write a short essay on Japan's history, I was amazed and disappointed that I could not find sufficient, satisfactory written information that would help me in the writing of the defense of Japan's honor against the many historical untruths written by foreigners.

This has affected me, and I am sure it has left a vacuum of doubt in the pride of thousands of our people. Many, including myself, salute our flag with much pride, but with pain and sadness when reflecting on our past history."

The old man was amazed and deeply hurt at his grandson's words. He limped around the room thinking, and feeling old and confused as to how to handle this critical and delicate problem.

5

He stopped, and looking down at Ito with saddened eyes, he went to cuddle him in his arms.

"Ito, I don't really understand all that you have just said. But I want you to know that no matter what others say, you should always be proud to be Japanese. Anything other than that will not only bring tears to my eyes but also bring tears to my heart."

The grandfather's hands began to shake uncontrollably as he looked into the face of Ito. "As you can see, I am now old, my sight is poor, my body has endured much labour and has many pains, but one thing, I will always be proud to be Japanese.

I served my country in our past 'forced wars' and even in my old age, I will fight for our Honorable Emperor and our country, again if need be."

Ito, looking a little peevish, knew that whatever he had said to his grandfather must have hurt him deeply. He knew that it was too late but he wished that he hadn't said anything.

"But grandfather," Ito responded, "I am sorry that I said what I did but this is the way that I feel and so do many of our people."

 "So please Ito, tell me what's in your heart."

Ito countered softly, "Grandfather, it's the foreigners' charges made against us which are very uncomplimentary. So please try to understand my feelings and that of the present younger generation. We are confused."

"Ito", he replied in a solemn toned voice. "Do you really know our history? Do you know the truth about our history and not what other foreign countries write and say to try showing the world that they are the good guys and the Japanese are the bad guys?"

He paused then looking into the boy's face, with a determined look, he continued, "Then please tell me what you think you know."

Ito squirmed and became fidgety, as he slowly responded, "Grandfather, how about the American anger for the attack on those sleeping ships in Pearl Harbour and our aggression."

His grandfather, feeling that his pride as an interned war veteran was now being challenged, tried to keep his cool, and with a pretentious smile replied, "My dear Ito, grandfather will spend as much time as I can to try to explain to your pretty head the facts that I believe are true of all the events that happened to bring us to a forced war. And as you say, to the bombing of those sleeping ships in Hawaii."

Ito, sitting upright, and with a smug look, countered, "I am sorry grandfather but I am really not interested. I believe that because of your great pride as a war veteran in his Honorable Imperial Forces, you will somehow try to counter my inner disappointments with words that will surely be prejudicial and biased. So please do not be offended as I do not have any desire at present to hear you speak further on this matter."

What do I do now his grandfather pondered, and with a passive manner, decided to appeal to his grandson, "Ito, this is not fair. Please listen to me. In fairness you must give Japan a chance to defend herself and in this way you and all of us in this world will know the true side of our story. Not just what others want you to believe to be true. So please hear me speak.

Some facts: the Hawaiian Islands were taken by the Americans in 1898, even though the majority of people were Japanese. The Germans took the Carolinas, the Marshals and the Marianas Islands. The Dutch took part of Borneo and all of Indonesia and Sumatra.

The Philippines were also taken by the Americans. Our Russian neighbors were not idle. They took Siberia, Northern Manchuria, and the Sakhalin Islands, which is next door to Japan. Portugal took islands of Macao, Goa, and Timor. Then we have France who annexed Indo-China including Vietnam, Laos, and Cambodia.

Britain, with the largest naval and maritime fleet, controlled all of India, Ceylon, Malaysia, and Singapore, part of the Island of Borneo, and many other places vital to British interests. Not satisfied, the British took Burma, and from took Hong Kong and Weiheiwei from China." Grandfather began to feel he was on a roll. He could see Ito slightly mesmerized and interested. He had rattled this information with a vibrant voice, while hiding his personal antagonism against wartime enemies, and in the belief that somehow he was talking to the world.

"So Ito, what are we to do? It was a good possibility that we would be next on their menu. There was not much left for these foreigners' to illegally take.

All that was left was Japan, Southern Manchuria, Korea, and what was left of China. We were really scared and worried that it would not be long before we would be invaded and exploited.

9

We had choices to either build our defenses strong enough so that in this way it might keep the foreigners out. Or better yet, act and be like those aggressive countries by building our armed forces and creating a powerful naval and maritime fleet strong enough to become like them and cause Japan to become a modern, respected, industrial country. Deep down we had no choice"

Ito did not understand everything that his grandfather narrated. "Grandfather, why did these foreigners take all these places?"

"Well Ito, it is like this: they were involved with one-sided beneficial trade for their countries, and they also needed low, low price labor. They needed ports for their naval and maritime fleets, and naval power to protect their holdings interests for their country and their people.   In other words, my dear Ito, it is known as exploitation with slave labor and greed.

You see Ito at that time we Japanese were in need more than any of these invaders. Our people were dying by the thousands through constant famines; we were a hungry nation with thousands of our people unemployed. We were over-populated with nowhere to go, and all these situations caused us many terrible internal disorders.

The future was extremely dismal for our people, with so many living on so little. Remember this Ito, the islands of Japan consists of many mountains, with very little farmland. And we live with a constant daily diet of earthquakes, some of which have been very destructive.

So our leaders and our great Emperor Meiji ordered the building of our naval and maritime fleet along the lines of the British Royal Navy.

So it was natural that for our best interests, that we trained our young naval officers in England, as the British at that time had the largest naval force in the world. This brought our two countries closer as friends."

Grandfather now became somewhat regimental, paced the floor, pointed his finger in the air and said, "Now please hear this important information without interruption, as the whole story will make it better for you who is so young to understand."

Ito thought he better cool it, as he could see that his questions and remarks challenged grandfather's pride tor everything Japanese. He nodded for grandfather to continue.

His grandfather took a drink of water and said, "What shall we do as a country? What was the answer? We finally decided that we had two choices: become a dominated country by the foreigners, like many of our East Asian brothers, or become powerful enough to be like the foreigners.

If you look at world history, you'll see the force of power enriched many countries. So we decided to be like the western foreigners, a modern country, and powerful enough to keep Japan and her interests protected, also it was fundamentally important that we take what was left of East Asia before the colonial and imperial western powers decided to move in."

"What was left?" Ito asked, forgetting to keep silent.

Grandfather continued, "Territories from China, such as the Islands of Formosa, Hunan, the territory of Manchuria, and many southern areas of China.

You see Ito, China was at war with itself. The Nationalist on one side, supported and exploited by the Western foreigners, and the Communist on the other side, supported and exploited by the Russians. As long as these two political groups were fighting each other they would not be strong enough to win back

Chinese territory taken by these Western foreigners, or territory taken by the Russian Communists.

Japan was influenced by need and fears to take these territories that were left for her benefit, rather than to let the Russians or Western Powers continue their expansion in Asia, or endanger the security of Japan.

To show you how strong we became, and how protective and worried they were, they forcibly demanded our government, in 1921, against the wishes of our country and the military, to sign a treaty to restrict and weaken our naval forces to a size beneficial to the United States and Britain."

Ito looked upset and with a loud voice asked, "How can we be so foolish to listen to them?"

Grandfather sighed, looked forlorn and answered, "They threatened 'Embargo'".

He could see Ito didn't understand the word so he continued. "Embargo means preventing Japan from receiving any oil, raw materials, and important good for our use, which we need desperately."

"Grandfather," Ito asked again. "Why can't we use our own oil and raw materials?"

Grandfather, now showing a little anger toward the thought of their forced Embargo, responded, "No, Ito, we must import most of these and the United States provided us with nearly all our oil. This we needed for our naval and maritime forces as well as for our industries and country. It was blackmail, so we had no choice."

"Grandfather," Ito countered. "It is getting late so if you don't mind I would like to be excused. I want you to know that I am grateful for your visits and information."

His grandfather also appeared weary; his hands began to shake, his body ached, and he was also ready for bed.

"Ok Ito. It is time to end our lesson. We will talk again." He wished him a goodnight and, as he was leaving, he hoped Ito would grasp what he was saying.

Chapter 2

The next morning Ito was up early and just full of anxiety as he awaited the arrival of his father.

"Mother," he shouted. "When will we see father?"

"I am hoping he will be here anytime now." Ito's mother responded. She moved about like a young bride awaiting her loved one's arrival. She nervously fussed and prettied herself to be a pleasure to her husband's eyes.

Ito walked up to his mom and said, ever so sweetly, "Mother you smell nice and I am sure that father will say you are very pretty." His mother giggled shyly and moved hastily about to prepare things for her husband's arrival.

It was not long after that his father arrived. Ito rushed to his father with open arms and poured him full of affection. His mother, walking behind him, smiling and with an air of pretentious dignity, greeted her husband, who while hugging and loving his son, acknowledged her.

They sat down for some tea and rice cakes and it seemed Ito and his father would never stop talking as they both seemed to have much to say. Ito's mother silently watched her family with much happiness and love.

Ito's father took them both shopping and for lunch. They had an exciting and fun time together enjoying the day, and hearing about his father's travels. They tried to absorb this precious time as a family for his father would be away soon again. Japan was booming and there was much excitement in the country.

A grand supper was prepared and guess who came to visit? It was none other than his grandfather, Kobiyashi. He came mostly to see his son, but he also loves Ito's mother's cooking and therefore endeavoured to visit at meal times if possible.

After a glorious meal and time together, Ito, his father and grandfather, left and went to the sitting area, leaving Ito's mother to clean up.

"Father," Ito called. "Do you mind if grandfather continues to teach me about Japanese history?"

His father, with a big smile, looked at grandfather with great respect and said, "I really have no say in this matter. It is up to him."

His grandfather acknowledged this privilege with nodded approval. "I am hoping that someday our Ito will write a book which will make all the Japanese people proud. I have but little time left in my old life so I must speak more often so that the truth of our country will be made know to all Japanese and the world."

He stood up, stretched his legs, and took a few paces. He sat down again and with seriousness continued.

"Let us begin. First of all Ito, Japan hated communism and therefore hated Russia. We did not trust them. They had great ambitions in East Asia, especially in Manchuria. Our Kwantung army in Southern Manchuria, worried about Russian movements in Manchuria, took most of Manchuria and established a state we called 'Manchukuo'."

"Grandfather," Ito pleaded, "What you have said bothers me."

His grandfather raised his eyebrows and with a sympathetic smile continues. "Yes my little boy, your heart shows pity to

17

others. But if we did not take or move into certain areas, then the Russians or the Colonial Imperialists' power would have done so. Remember Ito, we felt that it was our duty to keep all foreigners from their expansion grabbing and also to protect our country and our interests in East Asia. So we decided to pull out of the treaty on naval restrictions with the foreigners, which had been agreed upon in 1921, and face the consequences.

Soon we had some of the worlds most powerful and modern warships, and we were also on the threshold of becoming a modern industrial country, with much pride and devotion to the Rising Sun, and our Emperor.

Now more than ever the British, French, Dutch, and the United States felt threatened with their interests in East Asia. You see, they knew that their domination over these countries were illegal, but was safe, as long as there was no other Asian country strong enough to challenge them. Only Japan caused them sleepless nights."

Ito interrupted, "Tell me about China."

"I must apologize, my boy, as I do not know much about China. Someday I will buy you a book on this vast and one of the most populated countries in the world. So I hope that this will be okay with you."

"Please tell me anything that you know," Ito enticingly pleaded.

Trying to answer the demands made to him, grandfather Soichiro went into a posture of deep thought. He took a deep breath, waited and then responded, "Well, I will give it a try. Japan was basically at peace with China and had no desires for any kind of war with this giant of a country as it would be terribly costly for our country to be involved in a war of attrition."

Ito, with a sullen look, asked, "Grandfather what is 'attrition'?"

"Let's see, how one can easily explain this to a youthful mind. A simple answer to the meaning to attrition is when the manpower and materials are being used up faster than can be replaced or eventually unable to be replaced. So I hope that answers your question."

Ito nodded and his grandfather continued. "I will not explain why at this time, but in 1937 we somehow got involved into a war with China, whom we had had a close, peaceful rapport for a long period of time. The foreigners, who wanted to destroy us so that they could keep their illegal control and exploitation of Asian lands, went to the aid of the Chinese.

The French were shipping armaments and supplies to China through Northern Indo-China (Vietnam), the British and Americans through the Burma Road, north of Burma to China.

The Russians were sending their supplies from the extreme north of China, which borders their country, to the Chinese Communists, who at that period of time had made an alliance with the Chinese Nationalists to withhold their civil war against each other, and thus, help unify their forces in their fight against Japan."

"Sure a tough time for Japan," Ito mumbled sadly.

"Yes, but it was also an awakening to all of us Japanese people as to who were our true friends," Soichiro added.

Grandfather got up and paced the floor, and wanting to bring to the fore his contempt for the foreigner's actions, continued, "Ito, most of the supplies and armaments sent to the Chinese were not free. These foreigners not only made a lot of money in these endeavors, but their actions also helped to keep the Chinese poor.

If they could keep the Chinese busy fighting us, then they would be able to continue to keep their territories and their horrendous exploitation of China, and other Asian lands, as well as prevent Japan, who was then a new modern powerful country, from any temptation to move into their holdings and interests by weakening our offensive power potential."

Ito puckered his lips and interjected, "My heart pains for China and Japan, as well as all those exploited Asian lands."

His grandfather, a bit worried that this conversation was hurtful and difficult for Ito to fully understand, said politely, "Maybe we should end this lesson until another time."

"No grandfather, please continue. I want to learn all I can so maybe someday I may take it upon myself to write a book with truth about Japan."

His grandfather, who appeared hungry and tired, paused for a few moments and then continued, "Ok Ito, I will continue only for a few minutes more. When France lost the war in Germany in 1940, Indo-China was put under the Vichy French Government, which was a puppet government set up by Germany in France. Here was our opportunity as we were friends with Germany and Italy for many reasons at that time. We hated Russian

21

expansionist designs; we mostly hated Communism, which Russia exported to any country that was vulnerable to subversion by them. We were hurt by the treatment we received from the foreigners, especially the lack of respect, not so by Germany and Italy. For our security and interests our country decided to invade Indo-China (Vietnam)."

"Why Indo-China?" Ito queried with some hostility and compassion in his voice.

His grandfather stopped his pacing movements, drank some more tea, sat down due to some exhaustion and continued. "First and foremost, it was extremely important for us to prevent war shipments to China from the north of Indo-China. Next we decided Japan needed ports in that area for our security, and this area would also help provide us with huge supplies of rice."

Disturbed at what he is hearing, Ito again interrupted with a little anger in his voice. "Grandfather, I am not convinced that our actions were proper."

His grandfather smiled, and trying to be understanding of Ito's feelings, replied, "Let me finish. We took Indo-China with very little resistance, causing the foreigners within the area great concern. The Americans, the British, and the Dutch, decided to punish the Japanese because of its successes. They were worried that our forces now was so close to their vital interests, such as the ports of Singapore, Hong Kong, and Manila, as well as many other of their controlled territories. So they set up an embargo on Japan, as well as the freezing of all Japanese assets, not in Japan's control. The only way they would lift this embargo was for Japan to pull out of Indo-China and China itself."

His grandfather continued with much sadness in his voice, "Because we did not want more wars, we decided to make a deal with them. It is unfortunate, but we cannot survive without oil and raw materials. We offered to pull back out of Southern Indo-China and move all our forces to northern Indo-China, only if our Chinese interests would be recognized. These proposals were totally ignored by them and instead they made unreasonable demands threatening our security and interests.

One demand was for us to move totally out of Chinese soil. It amazes me that they showed so much concern for China, especially when they violated much of China's sovereignty, with France taking Indo-China from China, the British taking Burma from China, the Russians taking part of Manchuria from China, and many Chinese ports and cities given to these same foreigners as concessions of appeasement by China.

We knew that a war with the United States would give us success for approximately six months and then the might of the Americans would put us on the defensive, and not long after, crush the Japanese Empire.

Our leaders after much anguish and deliberations decided that if we must, we would go to war. We were cornered. One of Japan's greatest, Admiral Isoroku Yamamoto, convinced our leaders that we should bomb the American naval ships berthed in Pearl Harbor at Oahu, in the Hawaiian Islands, with a surprise attack."

Before Ito could interrupt, grandfather continued, "I know that you are not happy that we were forced to do this but remember: no enemy ships, no embargo.

We were the largest fleet in the Pacific, and after Pearl Harbor, we would be the largest fleet in the world. This would give us the power to defeat these foreigners on East Asian soil and get the necessary oil, raw materials, and food supplies for our people and industries. When you look at all the facts, there was no way out of this dilemma for us. It also would give us living

24

areas outside of Japan for our people in our ever-exploding, over-crowded population.

Many Japanese do not know that the United States, Canada, and Australia, had laws set in their immigration policies to slow and help prevent Japanese immigration to their countries. Embargos, hate, jealousies, and fear of our growing power by these foreigners, pushed us Japanese people to an undesirable conflict."

"Grandfather," Ito said with a surprised look. "You said we would lose this war yet we went to war. It makes no sense."

Acting like he was a university professor, grandfather continued, "Well, it's like this. We had hoped that Britain, being at war with Germany, and Germany rolling from one victory to another, would make Britain sue for some kind of peace with us, and the British might encourage the United States to go along with them on some kind of agreement fair to Japan.

We also believed that the United States would settle for some kind of peace treaty with us, as the American Congress, and the majority of Americans were strongly isolationists. Therefore, on December 07, 1941, we decided that we had no choice but to bomb the United States' Pacific fleet berthed in Pearl Harbor."

His grandfather, very hungry and exhausted from this discussion, was glad to hear Ito's mother calling them to supper.

After supper Ito went to his grandfather and asked him to continue with his story. Grandfather, tired and showing concern, said, "Too much history all at once will be too disturbing for such a young mind. I noticed that you did not eat much and you seemed troubled in deep thought."

Ito then pleaded, "But grandfather, before I go to bed, there are some questions that I have which I feel are very important for me to understand."

Reluctantly, his grandfather conceded and asked, "Okay! So go ahead, what is it?"

Ito, pleased with his grandfather's response, continued. "What I would like to know is what are your feelings in regards to the accusations of atrocities?"

This question sounded challenging to his grandfather. With a spurt of renewed energy he sat right up, prepared himself, and with a sterner voice of authority, he replied, "My dear boy, I hope that I will in some way be able to make myself very clear on this subject. The eyes of our people, and the world, must focus on not what always is said, but what is actually the truth.

Our Honorable Emperor, whether of the past or this present, as well as most of us Japanese people, including myself, do not, and will not, ever condone atrocities by any nation, including ourselves. But I must remind you that each country has their own standard definitions in regards to what they consider to be atrocities.

We Japanese people strongly believe that there is not a single nation that can honestly claim their innocence on these types of hideous actions. It amazes us how the propaganda medium of many countries never mention their own atrocities, but instead endeavor to divert the world's attention to the atrocities of their enemies, or those of other countries, whether they be true, exaggerated, or otherwise.

What we have humanly said is that we Japanese are sincerely sorry for any wrongs that our people have done. The doors of our hearts can only be totally opened when we receive similar and positive responsive gestures from those who have wronged us.

So what else do you want to know?" he asked defiantly.

27

Ito did not wait to answer and said, "Our history teacher told us that around the 1840s the British were the world's largest drug dealers, peddling the killer opium to the innocent Chinese people in China. I would be pleased if you could comment on this shameful action."

"Well, okay," his grandfather responded.

"These drugs were manufactured in British-controlled India, and soon found themselves funneled by ships to Chinese ports, and eventually, hand-carted to many places in China, against the wishes of the Chinese people and their government.

These actions by the British angered the Chinese government who ordered an attack on all foreigners, and the destruction of all stored opium, declaring the possession of these drugs illegal. They wanted only to help and save their own people from this brain-destroying drug, which eventually killed and made useless, thousands of Chinese lives, even today.

The British retaliated with gunboat diplomacy, shelling the Chinese till they pleaded for peace. The people of China were forced, by treaty, to pay a heavy price to the British in silver, commercial ports and privileges, as well as territorial benefits.

It did not take too long for China's anger to erupt. They saw only exploitation and rape of their dignity and country to these foreigners, so they retaliated once again in the 1850s. Unfortunately, for them, the British, with the help of the French, won an easy victory. This time they forced the Chinese to accept their demand that opium would be legalized for importation to China, as well as more territorial and port rights, including certain illegal infringements on China's territories be granted them."

"Grandfather," Ito interrupted, slightly angry now, "The British humiliated these people with their evil actions. What I don't understand is where were the angry voices of the world? Didn't anybody care?"

His grandfather was now more awake because of the seriousness of their discussion. He responded, "I don't think so, as no one came to China's aid."

"How come we didn't help?" Ito cried out.

"It's a fair question," his grandfather replied, "But unfortunately we were powerless at that period of our history to help anyone, so there were no ways that we could have helped."

"Grandfather, how come...."

"No more please, my dear Ito," his grandfather interjected. "We now must end anymore discussions. Your grandfather is totally exhausted. But I promise that I will be down to visit you again tomorrow, and if you like, we could continue to have some further interesting discussions on history."

His grandfather finally left for home, and it was a short period of time before Ito fell fast asleep, as for him, it was a long-drawn evening.

Chapter 3

Later on the next day, after a short nap, Ito woke up to find his grandfather in the sitting room. After their usual greetings, Ito somehow convinced grandfather to continue their previous day's discussion.

Pleased that he had somewhat opened the door to Ito's curiosity, grandfather began to speak more brazenly. "Now we will discuss the Americans. Did they not take a large piece of territory from Mexico? Was it right? They attacked and defeated the Spanish in Cuba, Puerto Rico, and the Philippines all in 1898 to help those people there to get their freedom and their country back.

Instead this is what really happened. They took Guantanamo Bay from Cuba for their navy, which they still occupy. They made Puerto Rico and American protectorate. They took the Philippines and never gave it back to them until approximately 48 years later."

With a disappointed look, Ito interrupted, "I am puzzled grandfather. First you tell me they went to war to help these people, and then you tell me they do evil. I don't understand all that."

"Well, please let me continue," his grandfather pleaded. "It is well known that thousands of Filipinos were killed or suffered in their battle of Independence against the American intruders. The Americans needed the port of Manila in the Philippines for their naval and maritime forces. They also forcefully and illegally took the Hawaiian Islands for the same reasons."

"I can see better why Japan was angry and frustrated," Ito said angrily.

"I hope you really understand what I am trying to say," grandfather responded. "Because of the foreigners' biased propaganda, the truth was never known. The only information given to the world was Japan was bad. We were the only invaders.

The truth is we only tried to expand our borders to protect our people from possible foreign expansion desires for our land, and also to protect our interests in East Asia, so we could survive properly as a modern nation.

Therefore, we needed naval and maritime ports as much as any other country at that time. The Americans showed contempt on our expansionism. They said we were not playing fair and therefore needed to be taught a lesson. Who's not playing fair? Is it the Americans? They have a Congress-approved Monroe Doctrine, which allows them to intervene in any Latin American country, if they pose a threat to the interests and safety of the American people.

The Dutch and the French were no better in their treatment of these East Asian people under their jurisdictions. When you write your book Ito, show the rights and wrongs in this period of history. It would show shame on those guilty countries, not just Japan."

"Yes grandfather, you can count on me to write the truth for all sides," Ito responded in a dignified, defiant manner.

His grandfather, in his usual manner during a long discussion, got up and started to pace the floor.

Ito asked, "Did the foreigners ever go out of their way to do good deeds?"

After a slight pause, his grandfather answer, "Yes, Ito, they did many good deeds. But the sad thing is many good things never blossom when evil deeds shroud their beauty."

"Grandfather, this embargo, can it happen again?" Ito asked with concern.

His grandfather patted Ito's head and with a scholarly look smiled and said, "Well, I hope it never happens again. Japan can never survive without the main ingredient – energy. So what shall we do?" Before Ito could answer, his grandfather continued. "Our leaders decided never to be totally dependent on others for energy, and our solution was the development of nuclear energy."

Ito, with a disappointed tone of voice, interrupted his grandfather, "Is this not a danger to Japan?"

His grandfather nodded his head and answered, "You are right Ito, but tell me what we are to do? We never want to be under the control of any foreign countries, so we had to go to using this dangerous nuclear power."

Ito took a deep breath and said, "Grandfather, why don't we use coal? In school we learn Japan has much coal."

Grandfather replied, "Yes, Ito, we can use much coal, and 10% of our energy is coal, but coal is more expensive and burns dirty. We are an overcrowded country with many industries. The heavy use of coal would destroy our health, our green lands, our water, and coat our beautiful Japan with blackness from soot."

With a disappointed look, Ito replied sadly, "We can't win, can we?"

Grandfather responded with a positive attitude. "We are trying to win, and someday Japan will win. Our scientists and researchers are working very hard on this problem. They hope to use the sun and the ocean winds someday for energy. In the meantime we have over 45 nuclear plants which provide us with more than 35% of our electric energy.

We have people who know about the disasters in Hiroshima and Nagasaki, and others who are against the use of nuclear energy, who protest peacefully, and others who protest with violence. The more nuclear plants we build, the more danger there is for nuclear accidents."

"Grandfather," Ito asked with a worried look, "What do you think of our nuclear plants?"

His grandfather waved his arms, sighed and said, "I see only that we have no choice, even though we have had some nuclear accidents at these plants, causing much danger, death, and injuries. Also we don't know what dangers lay in the future to our country from possible nuclear contamination. Our efforts, at present, should be to spend more money on the safety of nuclear plants and its operations."

With sadness his grandfather continued, "Japan has many earthquakes, and should they ever destroy one of our nuclear plants, we could have a horrendous disaster, which also may affect other parts of the world."

With a frightened, tired look, Ito said, "Grandfather, we must stop talking about all this as it scares me and I won't be able to sleep at night."

His grandfather, realizing he was not talking to an adult but to a young person, replied, "Don't be afraid my son. What I am saying may never happen. I blame an old mind, which is tired many years, and it sometimes makes me thing the worst. Japan is the pearl of the Pacific, and most beautiful, so let us look forward only to all the good things Japan has in store for us."

"Grandfather," Ito begged, "tell me more stories."

"I don't know what you would like to hear," replied his grandfather, resting in his chair.

"Korea bothers me," Ito replied.

His grandfather, a little tired, responded, "I cannot remember all I have said to you about Korea, so I will try to tell you more. Korea has many mountains, the northern part has many minerals, and the southern part has much agriculture, which is more food.

China was the dominant power in Korea's everyday affairs, and right behind her were the Russians. They both wanted to control Korea for their own interests.

Japan looked on and decided that because we also lived next door, we needed Korea for our food, safety, and for Japanese migrant settlers from our overcrowded country. Koreans are more like us than any Pacific Asian country.

So what happened? Our victorious war with China over Korea granted us total jurisdiction of Korea, including many concessions, as well as ceding to us the big Chinese island of Formosa (Taiwan)."

"Grandfather," Ito shouted, "All this is not right. To me it's unjust."

His grandfather responded, "Ito, you astonish me. The world is more complex than what you and I think. We may believe in this and in that, but politics, commerce, finances, and country interests, dictate people's thinking and movements.

If everyone one was like my little Ito we would have on happy world, with no borders, and no wars. Little boys would not have to be without grandmothers." He made this last remark in reference to Ito's grandmother, Kyoto, who would possibly be alive if she was not killed in Hiroshima during the war. He pondered what he had said and the hurtful memories of these past years made him a little misty-eyed.

After a long pause he continued, "I am sorry my Ito, but this old body must leave for home as it is now exhausted."

After his departure Ito was somewhat glad that the day's discussions were over as he was over-tired, with his body begging for sleep.

Chapter 4

The following day, Ito was greeted in the morning with a warm smile and a kiss from his mother, he responded with appreciative eyes. She then said, "As you know from your past visits to our doctor, you need to take some tests which could help you to feel better." Before he could interrupt, she continued, "So, tomorrow we will be taking you to the hospital where special doctors will try to help you."

With a disappointed disturbed look, Ito countered, "Do I really have to mother? I don't feel sick."

"Yes," she replied with such compassion in her demeanor. "They are not there to hurt you but will endeavor to find ways to make a healthier Ito." After a few moments of total silence she asked caringly, "Why do you look so sad? We will be there with you."

With mixed feelings, and a little depressed, Ito said, "Mother, will grandfather also come to see me?"

Know how much he relied on his grandfather, she replied, "I am sure he will try. You know, son, he is quite old, and his health is very poor, but to him you are very special."

Holding back his tears, Ito responded, "Ever since grandmother went to our ancestors, grandfather must suffer much loneliness, and I really believe that he needs much love from me." Ito paused, and with a forced grin, continued, "I do love him much, and feel boys are lucky to have grandfathers."

That afternoon Ito woke up from a little nap only to find a comforting face, weathered by father time, experience, sorrow, happiness, and love, smiling at him. "Wow, grandfather you surprised me. How come you are here so early?"

His grandfather, sitting beside his bed, replied, "Well Ito, your parents phoned me and told me that you will be going to the hospital tomorrow, so I thought I better get here before you left."

Ito grasped his grandfather's hand for comfort, and in a serious tone of voice said, "Thanks grandfather, you have in many ways taken away a lot of my pain, sadness, and loneliness with your affection, patience, and time. You are my best friend. You show so much pride for the Emperor and Japan. I give you much honor, but for me, I wish I could say the same. Right now I am puzzled as to what I believe, and what the truth is."

His grandfather, unsure as to how he should respond, said in a gentle appreciative voice, "Thank you Ito, you give me much reason for life with your concern and love for me. Even though I am old and lame, to you it makes no difference." He paused, held Ito's hands and continued, "You hate war and the evils that come with war, and to you I give back greater honor."

They decided to sit outside on Ito's father's homemade chairs. After some tea and cakes they discussed many things and just had a wonderful time together. When they ran out of conversation Ito pleaded, "Grandfather, please tell me more about China."

With a puzzled and surprised look, grandfather asked, "Why China again?"
Ito replied with some compassion in his voice, "Because I believe they suffered much more than anyone in Asia from wars and greedy foreigners."

His grandfather went into deep thought, and finally said, "Okay Ito, just a little history, because as I said before, my knowing of China is so limited that it's shameful."

41

Ito laughed and said, "Don't worry grandfather, what you don't know I will learn when I am bigger. And then I will teach you and you won't be so shameful anymore."

With a loving smile his grandfather continued, "Thank you for your kind words." He paused, and then continued, "Now let me see. China is a very vast country, and at the present has the world's largest population. It is predicted that only India will surpass them within the next five years.

Centuries of Chinese migration and influence has instilled some of its writing style, diets, culture, early manufacturing, and many other things, to most of Asia. This is very noticeable and well founded in the Korean and Japanese cultures. I am sure that you are well aware that we are now somewhat well received by many of our Asian brothers, especially in regards to trade. We have established mutual friendships and respect for each other that is unprecedented in Asian history."

His grandfather, embarrassed with his limited knowledge of China, said peevishly, "I hope you can forgive me, but right now that is really all I can say. But before you speak, I want you to know that soon I will buy you some interesting books of China and its history."

Ito, with a pout, and showing some disappointment, replied, "It's okay grandfather. You have always taught me that a little is always better than none."

Trying to change the subject his grandfather, still smiling, said, "Guess what? I brought you something special."

Ito, surprised and pleased, excitedly asked, "What is it? What did you bring me?"

His grandfather then proudly presented Ito with his selective purchase. "This is for you to take to the hospital."

Ito, eyes wide with anticipation, and with great eagerness, started to slowly and gently unwrap the gift, all the while believing it to be a toy kite. To his dismay he saw, instead, that it was nothing more than a Japanese flag. Unable to withhold his displeasure he responded somewhat rudely, "It's a flag. You already must know that I cannot accept this appreciatively at this time."

He thrust the flag back at his grandfather who was dismayed, surprised, and upset with Ito's unforeseen attitude. His grandfather then stopped smiling, and with a commanding but friendly voice said, "Don't' do this to me. I am proud of our country, and of our flag. You don't only insult me, but you also insult all the Japanese people and our Emperor."

Ito was going to interrupt but grandfather got up, paced the floor, looked at his grandson, pointed his finger, and continued, "When one gives a gift, it should be received with thanks and graciousness."

Ito could see that his grandfather was hurt so he quickly blurted, "But grandfather. I never said I didn't like your gift. I did not mean to insult our Emperor, or anyone. Especially not you, grandfather."

Shaking his head in exasperation, Grandfather asked pleadingly, "Please, then, explain yourself. What have I done, my Ito, to cause you such sadness?"

"Grandfather," Ito responded nervously. "You know my deep inner feelings which you promised not to tell anyone.

You have spoken much to me about Japan's and other countries' past histories. But like most of the newer generations, I find confusion in my heart to understand our past history, and our lack of national pride to speak out on the behalf of Japan's efforts, as well as the defense of Japan's honor."

44

His grandfather became emotional and also became misty-eyed, "Ito," he said with a quivering voice. "I cannot force upon you my feelings of my thoughts about Japan, but I know in my heart that someday soon you will be proud to be Japanese."

Ito, wiping his tears, looked at his grandfather's sad face and responded, "Please grandfather. I don't mean to upset you. I can see that I have hurt you again, so I promise that I will take this flag with me to the hospital. And I promise to display it when I feel better about Japan's honor."

His grandfather cleared his throat, gave out with a pretentious smile, and said, "You will find no doubts about Japan once I teach you all the true history of our great country. So please, let us not dwell on this problem anymore as it has caused much unhappiness for both of us. I will now leave you so you can rest your body and your mind and I will come again for our regular visits."

After his grandfather departed, Ito called out to his mother who was nearby hearing all of what was said, and was well aware of the happenings between the two of them.

"Mother," Ito pleaded, "Grandfather gave me this flag as a gift, and I would like very much to take it to the hospital when we leave tomorrow."

He was not sure that she had heard him as he headed for his room. He knew that this flag had much meaning to his grandfather's pride and for Japan.

Chapter 5

The next day his mother took Ito to the hospital. He stayed ever so close to her, knowing that eventually she would be leaving him there by himself. Fear was constant in his mind with hospitals.

Ito's mother was going through similar concerns and pains for her son. She naturally worried about any further negative results the doctors may find, as she knew recently from his doctor's reports, that Ito had cancer.

This health problem was known by all the family members, but not by Ito. They felt it was better not to say anything that would be depressing to a young boy who loved life. They were hoping for a miracle, or new drugs to cure him.

After the regular hospital preliminaries, Ito was given a bed. Next to his bed he saw a sullen face of another boy sitting up on his bed. Ito's mother left for home after she made sure he was comfortable, settled, and had given him lots of loving assurances.

Ito now felt totally lost. He looked across the room and there was this unhappy face of a boy staring at the ceiling in silence. Ito wanted so badly to walk up to the boy's bed and make friends. He was not sure how to tackle this venture. He had hardly any friends, and he really had not much experience in starting any kind of friendship, especially with a stranger. He thought that if he went up to him and smiled, that this boy might respond likewise. And they would be able to converse with one another, and, in this way, become friends.

Ito walked up to the boy's bed, tapped him on the shoulder, smiled, and said, "Hi! My name is Ito." The other boy sat up on his bed, looked away from Ito, and then responded, "What do you want from me?"

Ito wasn't giving up, so he put his hand out to touch the boy's hand, but the stranger pulled his hand away. The boy then turned his head, looked at Ito and asked, "Are you laughing at me with that smile for some reason?" Ito, who was puzzled, did not know what he should do or say. He became extremely nervous and wished his grandfather was there to help him. With a forced smile Ito replied, "I just want you to be my friend."

The boy angrily responded, "Why?"

Ito for no reason, laughingly said, "You're funny. Don't you like having friends?" Ito felt foolish with this gesture and remarks as he himself lacked the ability in making friends.

There was a silence for a few seconds while both boys stared at each other with challenging faces. Ito then continued, "I have to be honest with you. I have hardly any friends except my grandfather. You see, most people won't play with me because I am lame and in poor health. I am also small for my age."

The boy did not show any emotion to Ito's gesture. Ito, disappointed, sadly admitted his defeat in his endeavor and headed back to his bed on the other side of the room.

As Ito got to his bed he heard someone behind him. He turned, and to his surprise, there was this little boy stranger with a grin on his face and a couple of games in his hands, heading straight towards Ito.

"I am sorry for my hurting you. My name is Kato and I want to be your friend. Here, I brought you these and maybe we can have some fun together."

It wasn't long before they both opened up and had a great fun time. After a while Ito asked, "Why are you here?" Kato, without

49

looking at Ito, and still playing, replied, "Oh I don't really know."
Kato then rudely looked Ito in the face and said, "Don't ask me,
ask my doctors. I have been here a couple of days and they
give me all kinds of foolish tests."

With a fearful look, Ito asked, "What do you mean tests?"

Kato laughed, put his face right in front of Ito's face, and said in
a loud and friendly manner, "How do I know. They take my
blood too many times and soon I will be able to go home
because I will have no more blood for their tests."

Ito began to laugh to cover his fear of what he heard. He said,
"Good, I will be going home soon also, as I have not much blood
for them either." This caused them both to go into hysterical
boisterous laughter.

The morning of the next day a handsome, smiling man walked
into Ito's room and greeted him. Even though he was smiling, Ito
did not trust him, as he was afraid. "Hello, I am Dr. Ozaki."

Ito looked across the room at Kato as if to get his approval of
this man. Trying to be friendly and reassuring, the doctor sat on
Ito's bed and said, "I see you name is Akihito Kobiyashi on this
chart."

Ito was still afraid, not knowing what was going to happen next. He replied ever so softly, "Yes sir."

Dr. Ozaki continued, "Don't be afraid, I am your friend, and all the people here are your friends." And with a friendly gesture, nodded and left the hospital room, leaving a nurse behind. To Ito she looked so young to be a nurse, little overweight, but had a beautiful and friendly face.

She now sat beside his bed, held his hand, looked into his deadpan face, and said, "Hello, my name is Mitsu. I will be your nurse most of the time. If you need me or someone else to assist your needs, please press this button."

Ito did not say anything. He looked at Kato as if to get his approval on this nurse. Kato just smiled back, giving Ito some comfort to his uneasiness.

As the nurse was leaving the room she said, "By the way Akihito, Dr. Ozaki is an excellent doctor. He trained in Tokyo University, his mother is American, and his father is Japanese. He will make you well," and she left.

Ito was shocked. It made him terribly upset and disappointed with what the nurse told him about the mother being American and the father Japanese. How could that be possible?

He pressed the buzzer. In walked Mitsu. "What's the problem Akihito?" she asked.

Ito responded, "Nurse, please call me Ito."

"Okay, Ito, what's the problem?" nurse Mitsu asked.

"When will I see the doctor again?" Ito responded.

"Tomorrow sometime; I am very busy now so I must leave you," Mitsu stated and she left.

After some tests and boredom, Ito started to adjust to his new habitat. He was talking and smiling more and was more relaxed. "Hi Ito," Mitsu greeted him, "Tell me how you are doing today?"

"As good as I can be with all these tests they give," said Ito.

"By the way," she asked politely, "Why do you want us to call you Ito when your real name is Akihito? You should be proud to have people call you by your real name; after all it is the glorious name of our present Emperor."

A little disturbed with her curiosity, he answered with some sarcasm in his voice, "Well, if you must know, it's like this:

My parents, with my grandfather's blessing, named me Akihito when I was born. They felt that it was a great name for me to have. Our late Honorable Emperor Hirohito gave the same name to his son, who at that time was a Prince of Japan. Now that our Honorable Prince Akihito is our great Emperor our whole family, including myself, have agreed to somehow personally show our respect and reverence to his Honorable name, and that I should be referred to as simply 'Ito'. So there you are, that is why I am Ito."

She fussed around him, and smilingly said, "Well, Ito, to get better one has to go through our hospital medical investigative processes."

Ito did not quite understand what she meant, and then asked her, "Nurse Mitsu, can I speak with Dr. Ozaki?"

The nurse, busy doing her routine chores, thought for a moment or two, and then replied, "Why do you want to see him and what is it that you want from him?"

With a smug look, Ito responded, "There are things I need to know and I want also to have a talk with him."

Mitsu, moving about with her chores said, "Well, all I can say is I will tell him but you have to know that he is a very important doctor and he is a very busy person." And she abruptly left the room.

The next morning Ito heard some voices. He opened his eyes slowly and through his blurred vision was surprised to see Dr. Ozaki sitting at his bedside, with Nurse Mitsu standing by.

She stooped to fix his pillow and in a sweet gentle voice, "Dr. Ozaki has come early to see you so as you can tell him what is in your mind. So I will leave you both alone. Remember the Doctor has many appointments so do not keep him for too long."

After Mitsu left the room the doctor looked into the eyes of Ito, smiled and said, "Go ahead, tell me what is it that is important to you that I should know."

Ito first looked up to the ceiling, sat up a little, then moved his head towards Dr. Ozaki, and quietly said, "I want a Japanese doctor."

Dr. Ozaki lifted his eyebrows, stopped smiling, and waited for the rest of Ito's conversation, but Ito became silent. 'What are you saying Akihito, I am lost to understand your last remark?"

He paused, looked at Ito's eyes and continued, "Is it me you are talking about or some other doctor?"

Ito struggled to be diplomatic and said, "Dr. Ozaki, you are American."

Shaking his head in disgust, and in a serious manner, Dr. Ozaki responded, "You are but just a little man who needs to learn respect for older people. This is not your place or privilege to question or challenge me."

Knowing the doctor was right, Ito, in an apologetic voice, said, "Please forgive me as you are correct in what you say."

The doctor got up, stood by the bed, and seeing Ito's sad face said, "That is all right Akihito, and many of us say things that make no sense. You are forgiven. You see, my dear Akihito Kobiyashi, many Japanese marry foreigners."

With a big grin he continued, "I did not pick my mother, my father did. And I am glad he did." As he began to leave he smilingly said, "What do you say to that?"

55

Feeling uneasy, Ito sat straight up on his bed and replied, "Since you asked, all I can say is that I believe that mixed-marriages are wrong."

More surprised than confused, Dr. Ozaki, stopped smiling and with a serious tone of voice said, "Dear boy. It appears that you dislike foreigners, especially Americans. What you don't want to do is carry hate for anyone because if you do then you become a prisoner to hate. This is something that you can never be free from until you release this hate from your heart."

Ito did not respond right away but stared at the wall ahead, and with a smug look said, "Dr. Ozaki, my grandfather, Soichiro Kobiyashi, lost his beautiful wife and two babies in Hiroshima. Also, that means I lost a grandmother that I never got to know. Those memories cause much pain for us, especially grandfather.

In school we are told of these bombs the Americans used in Hiroshima and Nagasaki, as well as the terrible firebombs in our big cities which killed many thousands, of which, many were old men, women, and children. How can it be as easy to forgive when it is hard to forget?"

Ito now had visible tears which he was trying to hold back.

56

Dr. Ozaki felt pity and compassion for Akihito, and so he responded with, "I don't have to explain to you, but for your information my mother came to Nagasaki after the horrible disaster caused by the American atomic bomb to help us Japanese people. You see, she was a nurse. She met my father, who was a naval man in Japan's war effort. They fell in love and got married."

Sheepishly Ito looked down to the foot of his bed and interjected, "But doctor. It's wrong as we have nice Japanese nurses he could have married."

Dr. Ozaki could not believe this all was happening between a well-educated adult and the mind of such a young man. Ito now laid his head back on his pillow and stared at the ceiling.

The doctor then continued, "First of all, Japan would never be so productive today if it was not for the help by the Americans. Today our security and friendship is linked to the most powerful country in the world, the U.S.A. This, I think, is too deep for so young a person as you to understand but no matter what has happened in the past, we must live on, for each day is a new day, and each day becomes a challenge in each and everyone's life. Remember, no one is perfect. What surprises me is the concern at your age to all these matters and problems. You should be enjoying the happier things in life."

Ito still was silent. Dr. Ozaki, with a grin concluded, "I think enough is said so I hope that you would honor me as your doctor and we will try to make you better. I am also very proud to be Japanese and have great pride for the Emperor and our beautiful country, Japan."

Ito turned his back on the doctor and faced the window. Dr. Ozaki patted Ito's shoulder and said, "In many ways you are so grown up, but in reality you are but a child. I believe your confusion in all matters is caused by your anger at your illness. So I will leave you alone until I have to see you again."

It was not long after he left nurse Mitsu returned to Ito's room and immediately greeted him with smiles and said, "Hi Akihito, no I mean, Ito. I hope your talk with the Doctor brought you much joy. You know he was very kind to come early to speak with you, as I said before, that he is a very busy doctor. He is also well liked and honored in this hospital."

Ito just gave a nod rather than speak. The nurse then continued, "Tomorrow we will have special treatments for you."

Ito immediately sat up, looked upset, and responded, "Nurse Mitsu, what are you telling me?"

The nurse realized what she had just told him caused him to be afraid and she should be more careful in her response to him.

"Don't worry, these are very simple treatments, and your mother will be there with you. Today we take more tests."

What Ito didn't know was that he would be given chemotherapy with the latest drugs to fight the cancer no one told him he had.

That evening he sat at Kato's bedside, grinned and nervously said, "When we go home from this hospital I would like us to become good friends. We will write and phone each other as best we can, if that's okay with you?"

Exhausted and tired, Kato replied, "Sure, we will do that but right now I feel ill and would like to rest if you do not mind."

"Just lay here while I speak for a little while," Ito continued. "I am lonely this evening as I usually have my grandfather to keep me company. He is the only one who knows my real feelings."

Kato, almost asleep, mumbled, "What real feelings?"

"Sorry Kato," said Ito, "this I cannot tell you now as you are my first day friend. What I can tell you is that I am sad for our country's past sufferings. I am also sad that we lost my grandmother Kyoto in the war."

As he was talking he noticed Kato had fallen asleep. Ito felt foolish as it appeared that Kato didn't hear anything he had said. Oh well, he thought, why does he care how I feel. I guess grandfather knows best as he wants me to write a book to all who would want to know the truth about Japan's history.

The next day Ito was given minor treatments and later picked up by his mother.

Chapter 6

"Ito, grandfather is here" called his mother. Ito looked up with great anticipation, with eyes searching out for his grandfather's entrance. As soon as he saw him, Ito in a quivering voice, and trying to hold back his emotions, said "Grandfather you make happy days for me when you are here. I missed you terribly."

Misty-eyed they both embraced one another. Grandfather held him tight and said, "I am here my Ito. Like I always said, you give me reason for much life." Ito's mother Setsuko stood nearby now with some tears, as she watched the two of them radiating so much love, just like two little playmates.

Ito then whispered in his grandfather's ear, "Where were you? I did not see you at the hospital."

His grandfather wiped Ito's misty eyes with his bare hand and replied, "Sorry Ito, I was very ill. I tried; honestly I wanted to be there."

Sabaru call to them, "Come on Soichiro and Ito, our grand meal is ready."

They all relished and feasted on this special dinner, except for Ito who unknowingly, because of his body's reaction caused by his hospital drug treatments, found that he could not stomach food of any kind. And even the sight of it caused him some revulsion. The family had been forewarned by the doctors that this reaction to appetite is normal for certain minor treatments, but as parents they had hoped somehow that Ito would be the exception. Not wanting to show their disappointment, they kept silent on this issue during the entire meal.

Later that evening, as they were settled and relaxed in the sitting room, Ito approached his grandfather and asked, "Tell me more about Japanese honor please Grandfather."

Grandfather was ready to speak when Ito's father interrupted. "Ito, I have been listening to you and your grandfather discussing Japan's honor. So please give me a moment and respect me with your silence. Japan is, today, one of the most industrial productive countries in the world, and the largest in Asia. Japan holds the record, worldwide, for their quality in cars. We are the leaders in the manufacture of televisions, stereos, audio units, and electronics. And we probably build the largest heavy duty equipment in the world. We definitely have the highest literacy rate per capita in the world.

Our Japanese workers with our industrial corporations and the assistance and blessing of our Emperor and Government have shown determination and pride in their battle against the world, not in war, but in high quality and efficient productivity. We have a tremendous financial investment in the world. We are highly respected and friends with all people. We have thousands of Japanese living in the USA and Hawaii. We own much property and investments in American territory today." His father looked directly at Ito and waited for a response.

Ito acted as if he knew totally what his father had said, replied "you know father, you are opening my eyes to learning and you are affecting the misgivings in my heart." Grandfather please tell me again about my grandmother Kyoto." Ito now more demanding, continued, "It surprises me how you never say anything to me or anyone about your sadness and pain of the past, especially losing your Kyoto and your two girl babies in Hiroshima."

The old man held the boy close and in a sorrowful tone of voice, replied, "I hurt inside for many things. I hurt for my beautiful wife Kyoto, and my two little babies, Manaimi and Fumiko. I hurt that you never got to know or have your grandmother. I hurt for the

Japanese who sacrificed their belongings and lives for the Emperor and Japan.

But mostly I hurt when atomic bombs were used against Japan in Hiroshima and Nagasaki, which was not necessary, as a demonstration by our enemies of this deadly monstrous weapon would have been sufficient to end the war."

All this caused Ito to be quite emotional, so he decided to interrupt his grandfather, said, "I hope my love for you will cover many of your hurts. When I get big I will promise to write books of Japan's glory."

His grandfather pleased with his grandson's words continued, "Oh, Ito my wonderful boy, do not shed any tears for me, as it cannot help either one of us. By the way Ito, where is the flag grandfather gave you?"

Ito immediately pointed to his bed and said, "In my bag under the bed."

The old man lifted Ito's chin, looked his in the face and retorted, "It does no good for all I have said, and your entire Father has said, about Japan that you should keep our flag hidden. Is there some shame about our Rising Sun flag?"

Ito nervously responded with a whisper, "don't worry, I will show our flag soon someday, but for now I am tired and I want to lie down to sleep as it is very late. They then decided to end this evening visit, especially Ito's father who was eager to spend more time with his loving wife.

The next morning Ito's mother suggested they both should go and visit grandfather who was recuperating from his illness. When they arrived the old man struggled to greet them, and as soon as he could, sat himself down on his lounging chair. "This is for you grandfather, rice cakes and salted fish and mother said that she will prepare us a good meal." With a sympathetic look he continued, "I am also sorry that you are still ill."

Grandfather pleased with his concern smiled and said, "I am all right Ito, it's just my old body showing me no favors. By the way your mother told me by phone that you wrote a nice letter to your Doctor Ozaki. I am happy you did this."

Ito slightly embarrassed replied, "Yes, I needed to clear my shame."

His grandfather then continued, "It is a pleasure to me that you appreciate this doctor. Maybe now you can see the greatness and goodness of Japan." Before Ito could reply he added.

"Your secret should never have been born, when you weigh all things. Was it foreigners that looked after you?

No, it was your Japan. You had an excellent Japanese doctor; you had a wonderful caring Japanese nurse in a Japanese hospital with almost all your expenses paid by the Japanese people. This was available to you and all our people because of the concerns of our honorable Emperor and the Japanese Government. So what really is so hard for you to make a decision to be proud to be Japanese?"

His grandfather's voice had a tinge of anger which worried Ito, who replied pleadingly, "Grandfather, please leave me be. Today is not a good day to talk about these matters, as you must rest yourself until mother serves us with food."

His grandfather showed some signs of exhaustion, said no more, and decided to settle down comfortably on his lounge.

When supper was over and the three of them relaxed in the sitting room, Ito said, "I know that we should not talk about anything until you are better, but I see a picture of you over there in soldier's clothes and you look so young and good." Grandfather nodded, grinned, and responded, "Yes the picture brings me many memories. I told them I was eighteen, but I was only sixteen. They really did not care; they need many men for their arm. Oh to be a young man again. It was a new, exciting and challenging experience for me.

I remember how proud I felt when I was in uniform. We always fought with bravery, and most times, we were few fighting a much larger enemy,"

Ito interrupted, "My dad told me that we had the best fighter plane in the world in 1941, called the Zero. Is that true?"

"Yes Ito. We also had the largest naval fleet in the Pacific at that time.   This naval force was under the command of one of Japan's greatest admirals by the name of Isoroku Yamamoto, who incidentally planned the surprise attack on American warships berthed in Pearl Harbor."

"But grandfather, my father said that the Americans had broken our secret codes, so how come they let us bomb their ships?"

"Yes Ito, the Americans broke our naval code and our most secret diplomatic code long before the Pearl Harbour attack."

"If they broke the codes, then why did they let us bomb those sleeping ships?" Ito asked.

His grandfather now sat up, seemed alert and wide awake, and continued, "We must first look at the American President, Franklin Roosevelt. Here is a man who promised his people to stay neutral in other people's conflicts. The American Congress was also, at that time, strongly isolationists, which means that they only were concerned with their own interests, and mostly in their own spheres of influence. They made it well known that should we start a war against them they would severely punish us with an easy victory, which would take them less than three months to accomplish.

They believed that their powerful, heavy steel-plated armored battleships, with their destructive fire power, which was a big part of their awesome might of their Pacific naval fleet, would in itself be sufficient to keep us restrained and make us do what they say. Well, we shattered their arrogance and over-confidence with our surprise attack on December 07, 1941, which they forced upon us to commit.

We destroyed most of their ships while they were berthed in the shallow waters of Pearl Harbor, on the island of Oahu, Hawaii. You see Ito, the only way these big ships could be sunk would be by torpedo hits on their weakest points, and that would be below their water lines. Because of the extremely shallow waters where they were berthed, they felt safe from such attacks, as torpedoes at that time were not operable in shallow waters. But, before our planned attack, we had developed torpedoes that would be effective in such low water conditions. December 07, 1941, my dear boy was redemption day for all Japanese the world over for all the hurts, abuses, wrongs, sufferings, and disrespect that was done to us in our past 100 year history by foreigners, led by the United States of America."

"Okay you two, time for eating." Ito's mother called out.

During their meal, Setsuko gave a stern look at Soichiro, and said with an air of concern, "Time to stop this disturbing discussion. You are much too young to understand adult things." She raised her eyebrows, looked smugly at grandfather and said, "Also, you should not fill a young boy's head with so much stories about war. You must remember, today we have a good relationship with America. You should teach the boy more world friendship and help him enjoy things for a young boy."

His grandfather, a little aggravated by her remarks, looked at Ito, and with a forced smile, responded, "I guess your mother is correct in this matter, and even if she's not, I must agree with her, as she cooks so very good when I am a visitor to her home. By the way, where is the Japanese flag I gave you?"

With a tired look, and a negative attitude, Ito replied, "Somewhere."

Disappointed with Ito's response, Grandfather shook his head in disgust, mumbled something about Japanese honor, and said, "I guess it's time for my rest. But before you both leave I want you to know how much I appreciate your visit, your mother's cooking, and your curious minds. These are very enjoyable to a lonely old man."

Chapter 7

A few days later Ito's mother had some important errands to do and she made arrangements for Ito to visit his grandfather until she was done. It was natural for both of them to be excited with each other's company.

When Ito arrived the first thing grandfather was to offer him were sweets and cookies. "Gee, it's nice that we will be able to visit for a longer period of time today," Ito said.

"Yes, Ito, I also have a special gift for you," his grandfather said as he handed him a book.

Ito, surprised, replied, "You bought this for me? Wow! It's a book on China."

"Yes my boy, my knowledge as you know is limited in Chinese history, so if you read this, then you will be able to tell me, and anyone who will hear you, all about China."

With a childish look Ito said, "But Grandfather, won't this book be too hard for me to read and understand?"

The old man shook his head and replied, "This book was made for young readers, and what you can't read or understand, time will be your teacher. You see Ito, it's the same when I speak of Japan's history, because I know that many things I say, you don't understand."

Quickly Ito responded, "I'm smarter than you think Grandfather."

His grandfather laughed, which brought a big grin from Ito. Grandfather said, "It's well known that my grandson is the smartest boy in the whole world." Now they both began to laugh as they embraced each other. As Ito was walking away he notices a picture of a beautiful young girl, whom he recognized as Kyoto, his grandmother.

"Grandfather, tell me again about my grandmother, Kyoto," Ito pleaded.

His grandfather walked over, picked up the picture, and with sadness in his eyes, replied, "This lovely girl gave me much joy in my young years. I met her in Manchuria during the war years. We had wonderful children. You see, because of my war injuries I sustained, they stationed me in Shanghai, China. Shanghai is a busy port city with many canals and bridges, and is the largest city in China. We lived comfortably in the Japanese area.

72

When the war was almost lost I stayed in Shanghai, but for my wife and children's safety, I insisted they go home to Japan. At that time I did not know how the conditions were in Japan, because had I known, I would have had Kyoto and my three children stay with me. This decision and tragedy has remained with me almost everyday."

"Grandfather," Ito interrupted in a loving voice, "Don't be so sad every day, and you still have me to make you happy."

His grandfather sighed, walked up to Ito, held his two hands and replied, "Thank you for giving me so much love, which covers much of my pain. For such a young fellow, your words from your heart are a comfort for this old man. You give me reason for life."

Ito, trying to change the subject, asked for some stories about the military. Grandfather sat down beside Ito and with a worried look said, "Hope I won't bore you."

Ito immediately responded, "You never bore me."

"Let me see, where should I begin?" After some thought he continued, "I joined the Army at a young age. My parents were poor farm peasants, working the lands which we had to cut and level on a mountain. I decided to quit school, join the army, and earn some money to help them. Not only would I earn money but also be able, possibly, to travel outside of Japan.

After my military training my hopes of travel came true. I was to be stationed in Southern Manchuria. At this time we had taken almost all of Manchuria and declared it Japan's state called Manchukuo. I arrived at my base in June, 1937, and being a soldier, I looked forward to the excitement of being in a new country belonging to Japan. I was just getting into the excitement and challenges in the everyday life and routines of a soldier, when information sent to me from our military headquarters shattered my soul. It stated that a terrible influenza epidemic had struck certain areas of Japan, and was the cause of many deaths. Unfortunately, this included my mother and father, and immediate arrangements had been made for me to return home.

I was totally devastated and full of self-pity. It hit me hard at such a young age to lose such loving, wonderful, and hard-working parents. They were all I had. I felt so alone; somewhat like an orphan child. I then began to sob openly. After my parent's funeral, and a few days rest on compassionate leave, I was ordered to return to my unit in Manchuria. The unbelievable support, love, and comradeship of my buddies, lifted my spirits, which touched and changed my life. It was then that I decided that Japan's Imperial military forces would now and forever be my adopted family, as long as it was headed by our revered and Honorable Emperor. So you see, Ito, I had, and still have a fantastic family."

"Grandfather, I am sorry to interrupt," Ito interjected. "But I am becoming more aware as to why you are so proud to be Japanese."

"Please my Ito, if I may continue," his grandfather responded. "It was not long after my return that our military forces were put on full alert, and speedily shipped to areas outside the city of Peking (Beijing) China, where there was at any moment the dangerous possibility that an incident that had occurred on the Marco Polo bridge was about to explode into a serious war-like confrontation between Chinese and Japanese forces."

"Grandfather," Ito, with a look of concern asked. "Where is this Marco Polo Bridge and why were we there?"

"Well, I guess I should explain," his grandfather continued. "There was a massive revolt by over 220,000 Chinese in 1900 that went on an inhumane rampage of slaughter and attacks on all foreigners, and those alienated to them, including the then ruling Chinese government in Peking (Beijing), China.

Close to disaster and unable to hold back these revolutionaries, the Chinese Empress in Peking, and all foreign embassies, knew that their only last possible hope would be if they could get help immediately by rail from available Japanese forces that were stationed closed by in Manchuria. They begged us, we came, we conquered.   Our heroic Imperial forces were detrimental in the destruction of these rebel forces and their ambitious attempts. This period was referred to as the Boxer Rebellion by the foreign press. This is because the revolutionaries were organized by an influential secret organization of fist fighters, thus the term 'Boxers'.

Now my answers to your questions. We were on Chinese territory because the then ruling Chinese government granted Japan a 'Friendship Treaty of Appreciation', which ceded us large areas of their lands adjacent to and within the proximity of their capital. Also, all this would be under Japanese control and jurisdiction. The dividing line between them and us would be the Marco Polo Bridge which sits right outside the city of Peking. The Chinese forces were on one side, and our forces were on the other side. I hope that I have satisfactorily answered your questions and concerns."

"Gee Grandfather," Ito responded, "This is so eye-opening and interesting. Please continue."

"Are you sure you want me to continue?" his grandfather asked. "The subject is quite lengthy and may be too deep for you to understand."

"It's like this Grandfather," Ito replied with great enthusiasm, "You must not quit now. Your words have already begun to open my door to better understanding of the truth in Japan's history."

"So, let us continue," his grandfather replied appreciatively. "Evidently shots were fired from the Chinese side of the bridge, injuring our forces that then retaliated with more gunfire. It is sad to say and almost hard to believe, but this little spark got out of hand which eventually started an all-out war between the two of us. Foreign bias and anti-Japanese propaganda stated that we were at fault for starting this war."

Ito, unable to hold back his emotional concerns asked, "Did we?"

The old man shook his head negatively and with some noticeable aggravated anger in his voice, replied adamantly, "We did no such thing! Such ridiculous lies! We Japanese have a saying, and that is, 'It is very bad to judge anyone, unless you have faced the same experiences, and know all the real facts.' So please, Ito, you decide who is telling the truth once you hear the facts. We must first look at Japan's position at this time in 1937. Our military might was stretched to the extreme limits in protecting all our interests and responsibilities in Manchukuo (Manchuria), Korea, the Mariana Islands, the Marshall and Carolina Islands, as well as the Ryhuku group of Islands, not forgetting the large Island of Formosa. We were also strategically situated in many parts of China, which had been granted to us under Chinese-Japanese Treaty arrangements."

With a calm look, and his hands starting to shake, he continued to speak with more assertiveness. "So you see Japan needed all her forces to just retain what she had. Only fools would want a full-scale war with China. Their human numbers and their land vastness would devastate most countries that ventured a prolonged war against them, just by attrition. We could see this Sino-Japanese confrontation expanding, so we immediately approached and pleaded for the Americans to intervene in arranging peace between us."

Ito interrupted, "Why would they, grandfather? You said they did not like us, and I am sure they felt they owed us nothing."

"Not so, my grandson," his grandfather replied assuredly. "We believed that they had an obligation to pay us back for the many deaths and casualties of our heroic forces when we went to the aid of foreigners, which included them in the 1900 Boxer rebellion. How could they forget that it was Japanese naval forces that came to Manila, in the Philippines, to show support for the Americans in their war against Spain in 1898, in battle for the Philippines? Also, the Americans knew that we hated Communism and so we felt that this would be good reasons for them to want to help us in finding a peaceful solution to an ever increasing explosive situation."

Ito, who now appeared a little more anxious and tense, blurted, "So did they?"

His grandfather, showing some frustration in his demeanor pounded his fist into the cup of his other hand, and with a vibrant voice replied, "Shame on them! They did nothing! What upsets me is that history showed that they used us, abused us, were jealous of us, and believe you me, they were also afraid of us.

Our armed forces, which suffered and sacrificed their lives for us in their protection of Japanese interests, had at this juncture of time, no desire for more wars. They just wanted to enjoy a stabilized peace which would help in the enrichment and betterment of our people. We Japanese were and will always be a proud people, and we were now not about to accept any further disrespect and insults from some of these Western nations, including the United States of America, on our great country of Japan and its people. The many hurts that they did to us, plus their inaction, caused us much pain and anger which, as the world knows, eventually showed itself on December 07, 1941.It is sad that it had to happen but as history shows, they never took us seriously enough until it was too late.

Going back to this 1937 Sino-Japanese war, our military leaders decided that they had but one choice, and that was to increase the tempo of this conflict with a swift powerful aggressive force, hoping that this might cause the Chinese themselves to seek an end to this ridiculous conflict with some kind of treaty." His grandfather abruptly stopped speaking when he noticed that Ito was now fast asleep on his chair.

With a loving smile he lifted Ito onto the sofa close by, and covered him with a small blanket. Before he finally left for home he turned to take one last look at his grandson, and with loving admiration he mumbled, "Somehow I knew that this lengthy discussion would be too much for you."

Chapter 8

"Mother," Ito called out, "I wish I had a brother or sister like some other kids. My life is quite lonely, except for grandfather's visits." Before she could reply he continued, "I really should not complain because if he didn't have me he would be lonely."

"You are so right on this matter," his mother responded with much concern. "You have covered much of his pain over the loss of his parents and his beautiful wife and daughters."

Ito thought for a moment, looked at his mother's face, and with sadness in his eyes pleaded, "Mother would you please tell me again about Grandfather and his Kyoto. I only know very little."

"All I know, Ito, is what your father told me, and it is not a story for little boys, so why don't you watch television while I do my home chores."

"But mother, it is important that I learn more about Grandfather so as I can better comfort him."

"Oh Ito, your words are always so convincing. I really don't feel it's my place to tell you stories that I am not sure are totally correct. So, only if it makes you happy I will do my best." Ito's eyes brightened up and he eagerly waited for her to commence.

"The Sino-Japanese war in 1937 caused us to suffer many casualties and unfortunately your grandfather was one of them. He was badly hurt by bullet wounds to his legs. After the successful battle by our doctors to save his legs he was sent to a rehabilitation center where he soon met a pretty little young nurse, named Kyoto.

Her general duties were to care, attend, and comfort the injured that were sent there for recuperation. Her constant contact and attention to nursing Soichiro eventually caused them to fall in love with one another. Because of his injuries, Grandfather was given non-combatant status, and was soon shipped to a military base in the port city of Shanghai, China, for administrative and defensive duties only.

It was not long after that Kyoto finally moved to Shanghai where they were soon married. In the aftermath of many wonderful happy years together, they eventually had three beautiful children: two girls, and one boy.

In early 1945 things looked bleak in Japan's forced wars. Your grandfather was extremely worried about the safety of his Kyoto and the three children living at this period of time in a faraway hostile foreign land. With much sadness and tears, she agreed to return to Japan with the children where they believed that it would be safer for them.

As you already know, our Kyoto was an orphan child at an early age due to the loss of her family in an earthquake on the island of Kyushu, Japan. So she decided that the only place where she would feel comfortable at was with her best friend, whom she knew was still living in the town of Kure, which was only a short distance away from the big beautiful city of Hiroshima. It was not long after her welcomed invitation from her best friend to stay at their home, Kyoto volunteered her services to the war effort in the caring of little children in nurseries, and whenever she could, she would help out in Hiroshima's main hospital.

She was a person who had great patience and compassion for others, and sincerely showered her love, not only by her words, but also by her actions. She was a terrific mother and an honorable loving wife who always gave of herself. She knew that once the children and her left to return to Japan, her husband would be ever so lonely, and painfully would miss them. So to comfort him, as well as to remind him of their love, she prearranged for a single rose to be delivered to him at his military base, once each week for as long as was possible."

"Mother," Ito interrupted, "I thought that only us men send flowers!"

"Yes, Ito, that is the norm, but Kyoto felt that her husband had and would have his hands full defending the honor of Japan in those dark days of war, so she had those flowers sent in the hope that it would uplift his spirits in his times of loneliness. As well, they would act as a constant reminder of her deep love and affection. When the first rose was delivered, your grandfather was emotionally surprised and pleased with her loving gesture. Week after week those roses came and it was definitely a big factor in bringing so much sunshine to his life, and it also pleased him to be so honored with such good fortune in that he was able to have such beautiful children and an exceptional wife. Although he constantly lived in danger he was never fearful. He prayed often, especially to thank the Divine One for his happiness in the finding of the pot of gold at the end of the rainbow, which were his wife and three children.

Six months later, the world was different. In was in the morning of August 6, 1945, when the unbelievable happened. The Americans had dropped just one new powerful destructive explosive fire bomb on the beautiful city of Hiroshima, killing and injuring over 100,000 people, most of whom were women, children, and old men, which also included Kyoto and her two baby girls.

When your grandfather was informed of this atrocity, and the loss of all his family, he could not speak, and he went into shock. He felt totally devastated and he appeared disoriented. Not only did he lose his loved ones but he also gave up on his will to live. As the days went by, his anger at the enemy's inhumane bombing of innocent civilians eventually strengthened his resolve to get himself together so that he could somehow fight the enemy with revengeful ferocity, and thus, make them pay for their shameful senseless killings."

"It is so sad mother," Ito interjected with compassion in his voice. "But mother, where was Kyoto's little boy?"

"This little boy, who is your father today, was saved because he was ill and had stayed with relatives while Kyoto took her girls for a visit to Hiroshima on the 4th of August, 1945, to stay with friends she had met there. It is sad to lose Kyoto who was such a wonderful beautiful person. But you must know that she was not an exception, as thousands of Japanese women sacrificed their lives and possessions for the glory and honor of their country, Japan."

She then stopped talking, moved her face ever so gently to Ito's face, and with her small loving hands, wiped tears from his eyes and said, "I'm sorry my little Ito for reminding you of this tragedy. I have no right to disturb and make unhappy to such a young mind. I am always angry at grandfather for telling you adult things, and here I am guilty of the same thing."

Ito's tears rolled down more as he grasped his mother's fingers and replied sadly, "This story makes me very sad, but my tears are mostly for grandfather's pain. So mother you are not guilty for telling me this story, because the guilty ones are those that killed Kyoto and her babies." Ito then hugged his mother who was now also tearful and whispered, "Mother, I love you, but Mother, I hate war."

She hugged him tighter and whispered back, "It's good to hate war, but it must be the only one must have." As she moved away she wiped his and her eyes and continued, "Grandfather is so important to you in your loneliness. He fills your needs that your father normally would do with your father hardly at home, because he has to travel all over the world as a salesman for a large Japanese corporation. Now I must leave as I have much house work waiting for me."

Ito went to his room and sat daydreaming for quite some time. He then went under his bed, pulled out a bag where he kept his flag in. He looked around to make sure he was along and then slowly unfolded the flag of the Rising Sun. Quietly he murmured to himself, "Maybe I made a mistake. Maybe grandfather is right about who I am." With a slight grin, he folded the flag and slid it back under the bed.

Chapter 9

One lazy day while Ito was still off from school, he heard a commotion of loud boisterous voices outside of his home. He looked out the window and saw his mother greeting his grandfather and two other men, who Ito immediately assumed to be coming to help him in his research work. He rushed out, smiled as he bowed to acknowledge them, and with great excitement in his voice, cried out, "Grandfather, I have been looking forward to his day."

Before he could continue, one of the men looking at Ito, interrupted, "So, this is your Ito that we hear so much about. He is a handsome young man." They all chuckled as they respectfully bowed back, as is their custom.

His grandfather then began to introduce them. "Ito, my writer, this is Mister Hiroshi Horii, a Malaysian war veteran. And over here is Mister Hitoshi Shima, a China war veteran."

They all settled themselves in the living room where Setsuko set up sake drinks for the three men, which was only served in their home on special occasions, as Ito's mother did not believe in the benefits of alcohol. She made sure Soichiro understood her policy with regards to the limitations on alcohol refreshments.

After a few drinks and lots of loud, foolish, and uninteresting conversation, grandfather called out, "Hey big man, are you ready to take notes?"

Ito nodded positively, smiled, and with a shy grin, waited for someone to begin. His mother immediately excused herself after she poured them another drink, and then went elsewhere, letting the men have their fun and their male privacy.

Ito waited patiently for someone to start relating stories of their past journeys in Japan's historical involvement of the wars.

All of a sudden, Hiroshi Horii almost jumped out of his chair, which startled Ito, and then he stomped one foot on the floor, drank the balance of his cup of sake, wiped his mouth with his arm, looked everybody over, and finally turned to look directly at Ito. With seriousness in his face, he spoke out, "My boy, what I tell you is not exaggeration but the truth.

Furthermore, I do not appreciate interruptions when I am speaking, as in that way, I will not miss telling you what I want to say." He paused for a moment and then continued. "I was a soldier in the famous fearless Kwantung Army. I was involved in many battles, some against the Russians but mostly against the Chinese. In preparation for a possible upcoming forced war against the Western foreigners, I was assigned to a special force under the direction of Major Fujiwara, trained for infiltration purposes and designed specifically to spread disaffection among the natives who were held as pawns by these Western countries. This was done so they might rise to fight for their liberty and rid themselves of the while devils' illegal control, domination, and exploitation.

After our surprise attack on Pearl Harbor, our planes dropped thousands of leaflets in East Asia, pleading to those oppressed that they should not support these arrogant exploiters, and instead fight for their freedom and liberties.

On the evening of the 8th December, 1941, we were put ashore in Kota Bharu, Malaysia. We were dressed either as Malay people or Chinese citizens living in Malaysia. In this way we went ahead of our troops, by whatever way we could, so as we could pass rumors that would cause disruption and misinformation about Japanese advances and victories.

We worked and moved mostly at night, infiltrating into mostly Malaysian and Indian defensive areas supporting the Western foreigners. And we were so good with your false information that thousands panicked, lost their morale, and feared for their lives. Thus, they took flight, with many of them losing themselves into the treacherous jungles.

Actually a book could be written just on the greatness of our secret group. So I hope that some of what I said can assist you!"

He sat down and poured himself another drink, looked at Ito who thanked him, and pointed his finger towards Hitoshi Shima, and pleaded, "It's your turn Hitoshi."

Hitoshi, with war scars distorting his handsome face, stood up, paced the floor, pretended to be important, and began to speak with great dignity. "I was brought down from Canto, China, for the invasion of Hong Kong against the British. My Divisional Commander was Major-General Ito Takeo.

On Monday morning of the 8th December, 1941, we moved against the enemy. To us it was like hiking for a picnic grounds. It was so easy the first day that we took control of huge territorial areas from the British, and by the end of the day our Air Force was in total control of the skies.

We were also well-trained and prepared for movement on mountain terrain, which was Hong Kong's domination feature, as we were equipped with running shoes.

The enemy were dressed in full uniforms as if they were on parade. They were stupidly handicapped with their stiff army boots, which became a nightmare when mountain rocks were wet, and in Hong Kong, you have a lot of wet days.

Our troops had mobility and were trained at night fighting. We were truly tried battle war veterans, excellent in close combat and like storm troopers in our hand-to-hand battles. Our bayonets, which are hooked onto our rifles, are the longest in the world, thus giving us a tremendous advantage.

On the 10th December, 1941, we were totally ecstatic and energized with the announcement that our torpedo planes had easily sunk the battleships Prince of Wales and the Repulse.

In Hong Kong we found the enemy poorly equipped for a battle and ill-trained. It did not take us long to win a quick and easy victory against the British and their allies, who surrendered by the thousands.

How do you think we all felt? Japanese all over the world were proud and praising of His Honorable Emperor's Imperial forces. There were massive celebrations for our swift victories.

Now that the war is over many years, I would like you to write in your book that there were many enemy individuals who fought valiantly and courageously against us. That should be recognized, and so, honored."

Before he could continue, Setsuko walked in and in a polite manner said, "Thank you for this visit, and in helping Ito learn about our honorable country, but I think now it's better that Ito get some rest. It's not long since he has been in hospital." She acknowledged them with a bow and left.

"Yes, I guess she is right," grandfather suggested. "Time for us to leave, but we will try to get together soon again."

When they left, Ito made notes for his book, and listening to his mother's advice, laid himself down and rested.

Two weeks later Kato Tanaka, Ito's hospital friend, was a visitor again at Ito's home for the weekend. They discussed different events and information of Japan's post war efforts. They talked about plans someday to go to the United States of American, to maybe find some facts of the American side of the story regarding Japan's historical past.

Ito, knowing the possibilities that he might not live long enough to complete his commitments, tried to emphasize the importance of Kato's promise to write this book if for any reason Ito could not fulfill the task.

They touched on many subjects including girls, which Kato pretended that he knew it all. They had lots of fun together, laughing for no reason at stupid comments and actions, and generally behaving like little boys.

That night as they were playing Shogo (chess), Ito thanked Kato for some research information papers that he had brought over which had been given to him by his teacher.

"That's okay Ito, it's not necessary for you to thank me as we are both writers now and therefore all our data must be shared without fanfare."

Bored, Ito commented, "Let's not play anymore." As he put the game away he pleaded, "I would like very much for us to review and discuss this information that you acquired from your school. Is it okay with you?"

"I am exhausted from this long day of activities, so if we must, then let us be brief as time will be our factor. I hope you understand me, my good friend Ito."

Ito nodded his head in acknowledgement and, with dignified composure, looked at the written sheets then brought them close to Kato so as they both could read and digest them.

"My teacher says that his data, which was prepared and obtained for us, was the approximate figures of Japan's last available forces that would be available to make a stand on the enemy should he try to invade our homelands. This included Okinawa."

They both studied the sheets of information. "See what it says here, Kato?" We had available, approximately five months before the end of the war, over 13,000 Kamikaze planes. It says that these were to be flown with explosives on the nose of the plane for attacks by crashing pilot and all into the enemy ships."

Ito was going to continue when Kato interrupted. "Hold it my Mister Writer. Do you know why they called these planes and pilots, Kamikaze?"

"What do I look like, some kind of scientist? How would I know?" Ito replied laughingly.

Sarcastically and with a smug look, Kato responded, "I don't know about you Ito, but it seems that you have a long way to go, and much to learn if we are ever going to publish this book you keep talking about. Almost anyone in our country knows how this word 'Kamikaze' came about and it also comes from an important part of our history. You see, in 1274, the great Emperor, Kublai-Khan from China, demanded the submission of Japan – or else.

We refused so he got angry and planned to attack us on the Island of Kyushu with over nine hundred ships. But a storm with tremendous winds came upon them sinking approximately two hundred ships.

Emperor Kublai-Khan retreated and planned a second attempt with approximately four thousand four hundred ships. It seems unbelievable but the Divine Gods were with us once again and sent another storm with much more devastating winds which sunk over four thousand ships.

They retreated, never to try again. That was the last time anyone has tried to invade our land of Japan. We call that wind Kamikaze, which means, 'Divine Wind'.

Ito, in a defensive mode, responded, "I am still young you know, and I cannot know everything. You must realize that you are also two years older than I am. So if you don't mind let us continue."

Suddenly, Ito looked at Kato and with a sniffing, investigative nose, crinkled his nose, and asked, "What's that awful smell?" With Ito's question and his cringing face, Kato began to laugh and laugh.

Ito now a little upset, responded angrily, "What is so funny?"

Kato, trying to compose himself, answered, "It's my divine wind."

This caused both of them to go into hysterical laughter. When they settled themselves down there was an eerie silence between them which was broken when Ito, with a pious attitude, said sternly, "You know Kato. It's okay for us to laugh and make jest because our excuse can be that we are young and foolish. But really it is shameful and dishonorable for us to have fun on the bravery of our Kamikaze pilots and their loved ones."

98

This message made them feel guilty and sad. With smiles gone, they continued to research now with a more positive and serious demeanor.

"Look Kato, we had approximately five hundred and fifty one-man suicide submarines called 'Kaiten'. It says here that the nose of the subs had explosives which the sub's pilot maneuvered to crash into enemy ships. We also had over seven hundred midget two-man submarines."

Kato looked at Ito with an astonished look, shook his hand, and said, "You know Ito, if I were the enemy and had this information, I would be terrified to invade Japan's homeland islands, as they had destructive power of their heroic subs and planes to wipe them out."

"Even worse, Kato, Japan had battalions of human mines known as 'Fukuryo'. They were trained to sacrifice themselves by putting their bodies in harm's way by hitting their objectives with explosives attached to their limbs."

"How did you know that Ito?" Kato asked surprisingly.

"Because I am a genius," Ito answered in a humorous manner. "If you must know, I read it to you from this research paper. I guess we better quit our idle chatter and read the rest of this as it's past our bedtime.

It shows here we also still had the most powerful and the largest battleship in the world, the giant 'Yamato', a few cruisers and over fifteen destroyers. Sure makes me proud that we had the biggest and the best battleship in the world. There are many numerous things we invented and produced that are the finest in the world."

Finally, after many yawns, Ito suggested, "Let's pack up and head for bed." It did not take them long to be in dreamland as they were totally fatigued.

Chapter 10

Two days later grandfather Soichiro came for a visit and supper. Ito was really happy to see him. They discussed many different subjects, with his grandfather avoiding any references to book writing or to Japanese history, especially the war years.

Suddenly Ito spoke out, "Grandfather, my teacher Toshio Nagasone gave me these information papers about the Philippines for my research work."

Grandfather was surprised but ecstatic with this declaration. Trying not to break his promise to Ito's parents, he kept silent. Ito continued, "It shows that General Douglas MacArthur of the United States of America was derelict on the management of his duties, as many documented records show that he ignored all kinds of warnings and pleadings right after our attack and our bombing of Pearl Harbor.

He was advised and instructed to bomb Formosa's airfields as soon as the war started. Pearl Harbour's attack was December 7, 1941, and the attack on the Philippines was on December 8,

1941, which really is the same day as December the 7th because of the International dateline.

Here we Japanese were in real trouble on that date as our planes loaded with high explosives were lined up but grounded in Formosa because of bad weather. At this time we sat dangerously for hours, worried about an enemy attack. Formosa had the largest concentration of aircraft for war outside of Japan.

Still the American powerful bombers made no attack from the Philippines. Instead an order was given by this American General to wait. What to wait for? We will never know.

When the weather cleared in Formosa our Air Forces went on the attack, mainly on Hong Kong, Singapore, and the Philippines. Our basic targets were the destruction of every aircraft and airfield. In the Philippines we were totally surprised but pleased to see planes lined up like sitting ducks, some of them parked wing-tip to wing-tip. It was easy targets for our planes.

The planes in Singapore and Malaysia, including the ones in the Hong Kong area, were ill-equipped and outdated for air war and were easily shot down by our fast streamline fighters with their veteran pilots. Without air power they were lost.

My teacher gave us an example of the importance of air power. He said that in the Israeli-Arab war in 1967, Israeli's surprise attack on their enemy's air bases and airfields ended the war in six days. In these research papers it mentions the dilemma we would have been in had the American's initiated the bombing of Formosa, which they could have easily done. You see Grandfather, if the Americans had left their bases in the Philippines early enough on December 8, 1941, they would have reached Formosa about the time the weather was clearing up for flying and they would have had good visibility.

Can you imagine the destruction they would have created? It definitely would have made a tremendous difference in our take-over of most of East Asia, which in reality only took us about an easy three months from the first attack. One mistake by one General cost them terribly, and it gave us a temporary supremacy in East Asia and the Far East."

Ito suddenly stopped, looked at his grandfather's eyes and playfully asked, "Why are you so quiet? It's not like you.

Normally you become a professor and take the floor, especially when the subject is about the war."

This question made his grandfather a little nervous. His mind was being challenged as to how he could speak out without violating his promise to Ito's parents. Finally he responded, "All of this information you speak of is excellent history. What amazes me is that they glorified this General Douglas MacArthur during and after the war. In fact, in the history of the United States of America, no one has ever been given a larger ticker-tape parade in New York City than this man. Yet it is amazing that during the Korean War this same General in 1951 would be fired from his post for insubordination by Harry S. Truman, the then president of the United States of America. One can find numerous articles written that were critical of the General.

MacArthur's command decisions while he was in charge in the early days of the war in the Philippines. The foreign propaganda machinery went full force in making him out to be a hero, which eventually rewarded him with quick promotions. Looking at the other end of the spectrum, whilst in Hawaii, two men were made scapegoats for the Pearl Harbour fiasco. They were Commodore H. Kimmel, Commander United States Pacific

Fleet, and Lieutenant-General Walker C. Short, Army Commander of the Hawaiian Islands.

These two went through severe mental punishment with their own government investigations and charges, and of the incessant bashing by the American media. They were both removed from their respective commands, and in 1942, they were charged with dereliction of their duties and errors of judgement. Now does that make sense? Show me one great accomplishment or feat that General Douglas MacArthur did when the war started on the 8th December, 1941, until the time he escaped by submarine to Australia, leaving behind his troops to fend for themselves. He sure was some hero!

The British and Dutch were given to believe that their security would be strongly reinforced in time of war by the American Forces in the Philippines, especially by American air might. General Douglas MacArthur's error in judgement cost everyone plenty, but he was still considered a hero. I hope you understand what I am saying."

Ito, trying to impress his grandfather with his knowledge of Japanese post-war history, answered, "I do, but grandfather, I am told that General Douglas MacArthur was and is still revered by a large majority of the Japanese people. After the war years, he was appointed the Governor of Japan by the then President Harry S. Truman. He helped, almost by force, the Japanese people and Government, to rebuild the economy and our country, and insisted that we must always have a democratic society. With our own determination as a proud people we moved in such a short period of time, from despair and desolation, to become one of the greatest industrial and richest countries in the world. He was also a very faithful friend and protector of our late Honorable Emperor, Hirohito.

I don't know really what it is, but Grandfather, I feel that in some way you are still holding some bitterness toward the Americans by the words that you have said, especially in regards to this General."

His grandfather, feeling uncomfortable with his grandson's insinuations, responded defensively, "You are so wrong, very wrong to even suggest such a declaration. I have tried to teach you never to hate, and I personally hate no one, and that includes General Douglas MacArthur. What I really wanted you to know, time and time again, is that 'history's truth' is many times shrouded in biased propaganda lies, and that is why I constantly speak against it, and why I constantly plead for someone that is Japanese who will write only the truth of Japan's honor."

Ito could see that his last remarks had upset and aggravated his grandfather, so trying to be pleasing and accommodating, said, "Please Grandfather, say no more. I am going to be that writer. You have convinced me to write only the truth which, in itself, will shame those who speak lies."

Grandfather, who was pleased with Ito's commitment, thought that is was best at this time to change the subject, and so he asked, "By the way, how do you like your computer?"

"Do I ever love it! It will make my research work easier," Ito replied happily. "Oh, hi mother," Ito said as she walked in from the kitchen.

She immediately acknowledged the both of them and with an emotional tone of voice, responded, "My goodness, it is heart-warming for me to see you both together and I am sure you are both having so much fun."

Ito, grinning and looking at his grandfather, added, "It is not just fun, but exciting today. We got to talking about war and the reason why a book should be written."

Suddenly his mother's face turned ashen, her normal caring smile was gone, and she seemed hurt and disappointed. She abruptly moved to go back to the kitchen and as she did she called out nervously but politely, "Soichiro! Please to the kitchen!"

Soichiro knew that he was in some kind of trouble as soon as he heard what Ito has mentioned to his mother. He excused himself to Ito and followed Setsuko. "Please sit down," she said in an unfriendly manner. "You must know why we are here!" He did not answer her, but sat there with a pathetic and frustrated look, waiting for her to lash out at him. She did no such thing. Instead she asked him in a calm but stern voice to explain himself.

He immediately stood up, paced the floor, and abruptly stopped to face her. He now began to speak to her in a composed and dignified manner, "It is strange what one gathers when on hears only part of what is said. For your information it was Ito who brought u the subject, not me. His teacher, Toshio Nagasone, gave him some research papers about war, not me. I did not want to get involved in these discussions but Ito, with his pleading mannerism, got me to speak out.

The reason I spoke out was to explain to him about the power of foreign propaganda lies, and therefore my desire for someone to write the truth. It seems that I am always to blame. For what, I don't know! Somehow I wish that I had never agreed to your concerns as it seems that I am always the troublemaker. I feel that I am too old to be reprimanded, especially for what I consider at times, people's overreaction on trivial matters."

As soon as he had finished speaking he sat himself on a kitchen chair, and with a pout, he waited for her reaction. All was quiet between the two of them as they both faced each other. She finally looked down at the floor and in a passive voice responded, "Soichiro, you must understand why I am so protective for our Ito."

She slowly lifted her head and once again faced him, "You are aware that he is our only child. We constantly can feel his inner anguish for being one who was born lame. Even if he does not always show it, he is painfully being challenged by his health, and even more so for his life. Even though he is moving fast at his time to growing up, to us he really is a child. Sabaru and I are aware that Ito and you have a strong and loving relationship which has no measure, and that you both bring a special bond of happiness to one another. You both have shown great respect, trust, and honor for each other. Saburu and I want the best for him, and with one child, we are groping about without any previous experience. Therefore, I have come to the conclusion that no matter what upsetting discussions or problems that we may have, Sabaru, you and I, must always cope with it for Ito's best interests. So I will be first to apologize, and I hope you will now be more understanding of our overreactions."

Before Soichiro could reply, she gave him a big smile and quickly added, "Supper is almost ready, and I made some of your favorites, so I hope you are hungry."

Soichiro, with a stern look, got out of his chair, pretended that he was still in the military, and stood up erectly at attention, and in a loud commanding voice, responded, "As a Japanese soldier, our code was never to surrender, but in this special situation, I 'surrender all' when it comes to food, especially when you are involved in preparing it."

This remark broke the seriousness of the situation and it caused the both of them to break out into laughter.

Chapter 11

Ito's father was back home for the weekend. He decided that it would be a good time now for him to discuss boys and girls stuff with his son Ito, even though he wished someone else would somehow do it for him. He had mentally prepared himself for this entire delicate subject with the reading of certain books and materials, but deep inside he was still feeling nervous and uncomfortable. Also, Setsuko, knowing of her husband's anxieties, tried to add to his knowledge certain important information from a woman's viewpoint that she believed would assist him in his planned discussion.

Finally the time arrived with father and son in Ito's bedroom. Sabaru was fidgety and uneasy in his mannerism as he carefully explained to his son the reason for their meeting behind closed doors. He then began to speak for at least fifteen minutes straight, making sure he was not too explicit on this subject matter.

It was not very long after that Sabaru walked out of this bedroom and headed straight for the kitchen where he found his wife sitting there with a worried look. She was surprised to see him that soon, as she believed that their discussion should have taken much more time. She saw that he was sullen and troubled so she asked in a very concerned voice, "What's the matter? What happened?"

With a disappointed demeanor, He replied, "Nothing!"

She knew his problem was related to his efforts in the discussion of boys and girls with their son Ito, so she responded, "Nothing! With that face and pout how can you say 'nothing'?" She waited patiently for some kind of informative reply.

Finally he pulled out a chair and sat right beside her, shook his head in disgust, and responded, "I do not know really what I should say. I feel in some way that I failed in my duties as a parent with regards to our son's curiosity in his growing up. You know, for a while I thought that I was doing real well with my lecture, but then came the embarrassing questions from him, some of which shocked me. It made me lose my train of thought which then caused me to stumble, and believe it or not, caused me to stutter."

She was disturbed by his anguish, and trying to comfort him, said "Don't be so upset my dear husband, I understand. Why don't you just relax and tell me what else happened after that."

He paused for a moment, pondered, took a deep breath and continued, "Well, as you know, I have no expertise on this subject matter, so in disgust in my inaptitude, I just hurriedly but politely handed him all of my materials and books, and told him to please read them and also not to forget to study the pictures. With that I blushed and shamefully walked out."

His wife put her hand on his and in her usual comforting way, responded in a soothing voice, "It's okay Sabaru. Don't worry because I know that you did what you could, and also I am sure that all this had a great impact on our son who must have also felt awkward, but because he is Ito, we know that he appreciates all our efforts and concerns."

This broke the unpleasantness of the moment, and it finally created two grins as they stared at each other with lots of understand reinforced by love.

Chapter 12

In the following days, Ito spent so much of his time constantly into research work for his book that loneliness became a factor with all concerned, especially with his grandfather. Ito appeared to be obsessed with his assignments, and with it, he showed no interest in small talk or in his previous usual routines. All this was upsetting and hurtful for his grandfather who finally decided that he should visit Setsuko so as he could discuss and clarify his distaste on what was happening in Ito's strange ways.

Setsuko, who was also confused with her son's odd behaviour, so suddenly, welcome him. After some refreshments a frustrated Soichiro spoke out first, "So help me, I am at a total loss as to what is happening. There must be an answer or solution to this unbelievable disappointing situation.

This is definitely not like our Ito. My grandson is my breath and holds the key to my happiness which is vital in my desire to live."

Setsuko, covering her own concerns, responded, "Soichiro, do you remember that you once accused us for overreacting? Well, it appears that now you are overreacting. The changes by our Ito in the last few days do affect all of us, as I believe that it is only temporary. I guess what I am trying to say is that this will all blow over. Ito will be back to normal and everybody will be happy again, so we as adults must be patient."

Her words seemed to hit home with Soichiro as he finally smiled, nodded his head, and replied, "I accept your words as comforting and wise, but remember my young one, it is easy to say have patience, but when one is old, patience costs us time, and this we cannot afford as each hour and each day that passes brings us closer to our end."

Ito's isolationist mannerism was having a frustrating effect on the family, which they all agreed that they would try to ignore unless Ito's attitude remained the same or worse.

One day Setsuko, who appeared distraught, approached her husband with some surprising disturbing news. With mixed feelings, she told him that something strange was occurring in Ito's daily behavior.

Not only was he trying to lose himself from everyone's attention, but he, in many instances, was now also being impolite and acting disrespectful, contrary to his upbringing and to proper Japanese traditional behavior. Sabaru, now a little upset, felt that Ito's demeanor was unacceptable and also deplorable, so therefore some kind of action in the form of punishment should be meted out.

Being motherly, Setsuko suggested that Ito should first be given a chance to explain himself before any serious commitment to punishment. With her plea Sabaru could feel the vibrations of a mother's troubled heart, so he finally decided that it would be advisable to leave Ito be, for a little while longer, and if he showed no positive results then parental discipline would be necessary.

Days later, when Sabaru came home from work, he found his beautiful wife sitting in the kitchen gently sobbing. His impulses indicated that Ito was the cause for these tears. He caressed her and comforted her until she was able to respond verbally to him. She told him that Ito had taken down all his Japanese flags and dumped them in the garbage can. When she asked him why he just kept silent and totally ignored her. She said that she thought that Ito would be himself again like the Ito she knew, but it's not happening, and she absolutely does not know why. With mixed up feelings and desperation, she suggested that maybe they should take Ito to see a doctor who may help in understanding his strange demeanor. Sabaru believed that it would somehow be a plus if his father Soichiro got more involved in this matter. Setsuko concurred and a call was made to his father detailing the urgency for his presence to their home as soon as possible.

It was not long after that a sullen and tired looking Soichiro arrived. He saw their troubled faces and felt much sadness for them. Sabaru pleaded for whatever assistance that his father could provide in trying to open the door to Ito's puzzling mindset. They believed that both Ito and his grandfather have a special bonding, reinforced by their closeness, love, respect and friendship, and thus they could better understand and speak to each other in their own language.

Feeling important by their request, Soichiro agreed. They patiently and nervously waited for Ito's return to their home from school. When he arrived and saw their grim faces, stamped with artificial smiles, he knew that he must be the focus of their attention due to his unexplainable behavior, and sensing a possible confrontation, he politely acknowledged them. Before any one of them could speak, he headed straight for his bedroom.

Sabaru, full of anxiety, and wanting to get this problem resolved as soon as possible, followed Ito to his room. After a few minutes went by Sabaru rushed out and headed for the kitchen where Setsuko and his father were patiently waiting for him. He then threw his hands up in the air, shrugged his shoulders, and showing disgust and frustration, he stammered loudly, "I give up! Discipline and punishment is a must in this situation."

He then turned to look directly at his wife, and continued, "I ask only that we do not lean on empathy to erase his deplorable mannerism. We must, as parents, redress our son properly while he is still young and where there is still hope. We must be careful that we do not let our hearts spare him for his disrespect even if he becomes tearful."

He paused, shook his head negatively, and said, "Our Ito defiantly objected to any family meeting claiming that he was presently in no position to want to talk about all of our concerns due to his health, and most importantly, he emphasised with some anger, that he definitely had no desire for any personal communication with her grandfather at this time."

This was a sad dilemma for all of them. Grandfather Soichiro would not let himself believe what he had just heard, even though he had hurt feelings. This was too shocking for him to accept, and caused him some depression.

He finally spoke out, "I must go and confront my grandson on this serious matter, and I also would like to know why he singled me out on his objection. I have done nothing to cause his displeasure with me."

As he made a move to go to Ito's room, a worried Setsuko grabbed his arm gently and spoke pleadingly, like most compassionate mothers, "Please Soichiro, I ask only that you would try to be patient and understanding with our little Ito, he needs all our support."

Grandfather Soichiro rapped on Ito's bedroom door. There was no response. So he just walked in uninvited, where he saw an unhappy boy lying down on his bed with his school clothes still on, staring at the ceiling, "Hi! What's wrong?" Soichiro asked pleadingly. Ito did not move or respond and showed no emotion. "Please Ito, this is me, Grandfather! Your best friend, remember? Please speak; this silence is childish and ridiculous, especially between us."

He finally sat on one side of Ito's bed where he noticed tears starting to blur Ito's vision. They both sat silently for a while, when Ito slowly sat up, looked at his grandfather squarely in his face, and then with tears now very visible rolling down his cheeks, he answered angrily, "I am finished with my ambition to write a a book in Japan's honor."

This remark astounded his grandfather, who immediately stood up, and with a troubled heart, waited to hear what else his grandson had to say.

Wiping his eyes with his hands and his shirtsleeves, Ito continued, "You see, I did my research work, and to my surprise I found much information that contradicts much of what you have told me about our Japan and its people. I am in doubt as to who is really guilty in starting the Sino-Japanese war that began at the Marco Polo Bridge, in China, in 1937. Also, the Americans claimed that they did the right thing when they dropped atomic bombs on Hiroshima and Nagasaki, as it helped shorten the war, thus averting additional unnecessary casualties and destruction.

Speaking more aggressively, Ito continued, "You said that the invasion of Korea, Manchuria and other territories were necessary for our survival and exploding population. Then how come we are such a rich, productive country today, with about three times more people, and without the need of invading or occupying any foreign territories."

He could see his grandfather wanting to speak but Ito had to keep going, "You always said that we should never hate, and must speak only the truth, so Grandfather, I ask, where do you stand on the truth?"

Soichiro, a little choked up, and weighted down by exhaustion, answered diplomatically, "How can I explain myself so that you will grasp and understand the depth of my beliefs, and the reasons for all that really has happened in our history of Japan and the Japanese people. You have said things that many in the world believe, but I want you to know that I will defend the untruths forever, in Japan's honor. In the first place, where did you get most of your information? Before you even have to answer, I will tell you where, you got them from books, your computer, and the media, which everyone knows are controlled by foreigners, some of whom dominate the news world with their tremendous financial and world power. Remember this, my dear Ito, wealth makes lots of friends, but the poor is unfairly separated from his neighbors."

As he paused to take a deep breath, Ito rudely, but unintentionally, interrupted, "You should hear this then, grandfather. My teacher wrote this down for me, which I would like to read to you. 'Before honor must come truth with humility. History teaches us where we came from and who we really are, and with it the pride of what we accomplished, but we must tell the truth of what we did wrong, so that we can learn from it, otherwise we may walk deaf and blind towards a destructive tomorrow.' So, Grandfather, I ask only that you do not belittle the facts."

His grandfather, Soichiro, feeling the pain that comes with old age and with the discomfort of some kind of malaise, responded apologetically, "Do not worry, I will endeavor to be more informative, but now is not a good time for us to continue this discussion, as I feel overwhelmed by all this, which has caused me much physical and mental strain.

Rather than any verbal answers to your questions and concerns, I will instead respond to all these matters in the written form. I also hope that you will cease any of your antagonism or any of your deplorable behavior, as this is totally unacceptable and disrespectful to all of us, and is not the proper mannerism for one so young, especially in the code of ethics demanded by our Japanese society."

Ito, with a dismal look and a pout, replied in a reluctant manner, "I will obey your wishes and also to all those who are concerned, but I want you to know that until such time as you can prove the foreigners are wrong, or they have exaggerated their accusations, I will want nothing to do with Japanese history."

"What you have just said is shameful to our Emperor and the Japanese people, as you have unfairly made your decisions without giving me the chance to prove the truth of Japan's honor," his grandfather angrily responded on his way out of Ito's room.

As soon as Socichiro entered the living room, Ito's parents, who were sitting there with sullen faces, and tense with anxiety, greeted him. He immediately explained in brief what was said and what had happened, which helped to reduce their tensions and calmed their parental concerns. All the while, Sabaru noticed his father's movement and speech were slow, and his appearance was not normal, suggesting Soichiro should head for home right away for a much needed rest. They would meet again at a more appropriate time to digest and explore all that was discussed between Soichiro and their son, Ito.

Ito had remained in his room until he was called for supper. Other than Ito's apology for his unacceptable behavior to his parents, which was accepted by them, there was only a few words spoken at the table. When they were finished, Ito excused himself, and before they could acknowledge his leaving, he got up and began to head out of the kitchen.

Ito's movement ceased when his father bellowed, "Not so fast, my son. You are forgiven for your shameful actions but it is our duty as parents to discipline you by setting up some kind of punishment. Before I speak further, I would like you to briefly explain yourself in regards to your improper mannerisms."

Ito noticed their eyes were troubled, their faces distraught, which held him up from immediately speaking. He thought for a few seconds, preparing his mind to properly respond to their concerns. He finally spoke out, "I will always love my grandfather, and I know that he will always love me. If you remember, there was a time that I was not proud and had mixed feelings on our past history, but because grandfather, Soichiro, is a proud war veteran who always defends the honor of the

Emperor and the Japanese people, he did all he could to convince me that it was wrong and shameful to act and think like that. He succeeded and I became gung-ho for everything Japanese, to the point that I wanted to be the one who would write the truth of our one hundred years history in Japan's honor. I had lots of help and encouragement from many people, but mostly from my grandfather. All this responsibility and challenge made me feel important and special. While I was doing my research work I found much information that contradicted what I was told, most of which was given or told to me by my grandfather. This also destroyed my desire to write. At any rate, until Grandfather can give me satisfactory answers, I would like to be left alone with my thoughts, which at the present time, are causing me much mental strain."

He paused long enough to let them know that he was finished speaking. Sabaru then got up from his chair and began to pace the floor, in similar fashion as his father Soichiro seem to do whenever he was tense and wanted to speak with forcefulness on any subject matters that appeared to be of great importance. He finally stepped in front of Ito, looked right at his face, and in a commanding parental voice, said, "What you have spoken shows us that you had many personal reasons for your strange behavior, but disrespect is not excusable at any time in your upbringing. Therefore, you are to be grounded for one week without the privileges of television viewing, and the use of your computer. You will also lose all your allowance for one whole month, starting as of now. You have permission to leave, as that is all I have to say."

An unhappy, disgruntled Ito headed for his bedroom with his mother following right behind him. As soon as they were alone she held his hands and, in her usual caring way, said, "I am disturbed and sorry that all this had to happen as you know how much we love you. We hate to see you punished. You must know that when Ito hurts, we hurt."

Ito, looking at his mother's beautiful face, gave a slight grin of appreciation and responded, "Thanks Mother, you always are a comfort to me, which, at times like this, helps to ease some of my pain and frustrations.

The world has many who protest against the world's wrongs. They sincerely believe in their caused, but unfortunately there are many who accuse them of being troublemakers, claiming that they are ignorant of their causes and that they are also lacking proper information. I am totally against anyone who punishes them for their beliefs, except for those who go beyond their beliefs disregarding 'Law and Order' in their actions. Therefore, Mother, after all what I have spoken, I want you to know that I accept my punishment which was necessitated when I broke the law and order of our home."

Chapter 13

The next day his mother gave him a large envelope from his grandfather. Ito immediately sensed that the contents would be information in regards to the defense of Japan.

As soon as he could he headed to the privacy of his room, where he nervously opened it, took the written sheets out and began to read:

> To my dearest grandson Ito,
>
> How should I begin? How can I be convincing? Maybe you think that somehow I may have an ulterior motive in my defensive words and action for our Japan. You may also feel that I do not have the ability and qualifications to speak on behalf of our Emperor and our people, especially since I only had a very low grade of education. I want you to believe me when I say that time and determination to learn can improve one's education and knowledge.

Not long after the war my comrades and I shipped back to Japan. We were all ecstatic, elated, and ever so thankful to be going back to our motherland. It was natural that many of us became tearful when we finally docked.

Although happy to be home, many of us were somewhat saddened by the nostalgic past memories of our glorious days. When we arrived we expected to be welcomed by homecoming bands, cheering crowds of enthusiastic people, and loved ones anxiously waiting to greet us. Instead, there was just dismal silence and emptiness. Our thoughts were interrupted by reality, as the American victors, whom we still felt was the enemy, processed us for landing and for departure arrangements made to our individual destinations.

I wanted everyone to know that I, Soichiro Kobiyashi, was a proud soldier of the Imperial Forces, and no matter what the circumstances, whether it is good or bad, I shall always walk tall to the honor of my country. So it was only natural that I was dressed and ready to travel in my military uniform, even though it was now torn, tattered, and stained with sweat, blood, and dirt.

As I travelled, I saw mile after mile of terrible destruction. It seemed to me that whenever I saw people, I saw sadness, poverty, and hunger. Many shunned any uniformed Japanese and there were many who blamed us for Japan's downfall and the plight of the people. In plain language, we were not welcomed home.

What I do not understand is why they tried to belittle and shame me when they must have known that, as a soldier, I had put my life in harm's way for our Emperor and the Japanese people.

They somehow must have considered me as a loser and, because the war was over, unimportant. This personally affected me and caused me much pain and anguish. Whatever happened to our honorable Japanese people who, for more than one hundred years, acknowledged and venerated the Emperor and all his Majesty's Imperial Forces?

I felt the lease they could do was to show some appreciative grateful gestures. At any rate, I was determined not to let my valor and pride take a back seat to anyone.

130

All this did not deter me from my main goal, which was to proceed to the city of Hiroshima where my wife and children had been killed.

When I arrived, the destruction was so total that it shocked me into a hysterical state of mental depression. I began to cry and cry. I yelled their names over and over again in the hope that I would somehow hear them respond. At that time I was not aware that my son was still alive, in the care of Kyoto's good friends in Kure. I was such a lost soul helplessly alone. I desperately wanted to see Kyoto and my beautiful son.

I began to think suicide, as in that way I could be together as a family again. I was suddenly brought to reality by some strange inner voice that took total control of me. It commanded me to settle down and to go forward in my life. Then there was a total eerie silence. I stared at the emptiness of Hiroshima and finally cried out in a loud voice, "Why Hiroshima?" This question became a challenge call and an obsession to me. You will be surprised to know that it forced me to do research work on Japan's one hundred years of history, which eventually took me over ten years of investigative work.

Now you can see that I have some credentials. Therefore, my dearest Ito, on behalf of our honorable Emperor and the Japanese people, I beg you to pay serious attention to all what I have to say. I am praying my words, which reflect the truth, may open your heart in accepting the greatness of Japan. I am also praying that somehow this power of the Divine One will make you have the desire again to want to write the book in truth about Japan's honor.

I am writing in such a way that I may be able to explain as to who we really are, why we are, the way we are, what happened to us, and the reasons for all that has happened, including the present history of today's Japan.

I am certain that when I'm finished with only the truth in Japan's defense, it will convince the world, our people, and you, of the terrible actions and injustices done to us; especially by the foreign propaganda lies, and their derogatory and discriminating remarks.

I am asking the whole world as well as the Japanese people to understand all what I have to say, so that in the end we will gain back the respect, glory, and honor, which is rightly ours.

If at the conclusion of my defense, one is convinced that what is written is true, and without any doubts believable, then one should show compassion, forgiveness if need be, and understanding for our Emperor and for all the Japanese people, past and present.

Who are we? History mentions that we are a mixture of Korean, Chinese, and the Indigenous Ainu people. Our islands were dominated and exploited by warlords who were in constant battle with one another. This was Japan's feudal system, a country constantly engulfed in some kind of violence with the brunt affecting the poor peasants.

Then history tells us of a special breed call the Samurais, which means 'one who serves'. Their code demanded absolute loyalty to their superiors. Family was never to interfere in their commitments. They were taught to never fear dangers or death. With their teachings, war was their aim, and that one must kill or be killed. They trained in the art of war at an early age to become such great warriors. Their 'Bushido' scared code says, 'a Samurai should live and die with his sword in his hand'.

The last of the Samurais ended in 1877 (just sixty-four years before the forced attack on Pearl Harbor) when conscripts created by the Emperor Meiji defeated a Samurai revolt. From then on the people wanted a stronger military government ruled over by an emperor. We Japanese people believe that without an emperor we would be without a country, as he represents our Empire and our flag. He is like a father who loves and guides us. We venerate and respect him highly.

Did you know that with the guidance of our Emperor, Meiji, and the determined efforts of our military and people, we transformed ourselves from an isolated country to an industrial world power, with a strong army and a powerful navel and maritime fleet? This amazing feat took less than fifty years, which unfortunately caused many jealousies, fear, and hate towards our people by numerous countries.

I am sure that we all can agree that militarism played a dominant role in our history. Our people's loyalty and love of the country accepted the fact that to die in peace or in war is the destiny of every person and the living should take that to heart.

Please try to understand what is being said regarding the military. It is important at this time that you withhold any criticisms or judgements until such time that I will have fully completed my defense. My information from our history suggests that war, uprisings, revolts, and violence, were a norm from generation to generation, and therefore, there should be no surprises to the world to better understand us, as our past had in a big way influenced our future.

To give his mental mind a time out, Ito temporarily stopped reading. It seemed that girl next door had in some way much to do with his concentration. He realized that what was in front of him was extremely important and that someday it will surely be a factor in the battle for the truth of Japan's history, whereas the girl next door is only a slight interruption of time. In all fairness to his grandfather's investigative work, Ito decided that it was a

must for total attention on the matter set before him, so he
continued to read:

> Now I will endeavor to show the world and
> you why the   Japanese people had so much anger, and
> in many instances, hate for the foreigners. So let me
> explain hate. It is the accumulation of anger that
> eventually becomes a dangerous uncontrollable
> explosive force.
>
> Our anger really began when the Americans,
> British, French, Russian, and Dutch navies used threats
> and actual force to break open the door to Japan's
> isolationism, with the foreigners demanding and obtaining
> Port Treaties and beneficial concessions for themselves.
> They made us realize how defenseless we were. They
> did this in a period of approximately eighteen years, from
> 1846 – 1864. So I ask the people of the world – was this
> not aggression? Were they not the aggressors? As a
> people would that not make you angry?
>
> At any rate, what did their actions teach us? It
> openly said, "If you have power, you can take or demand
> from the weak and defenseless whatever pleases you."

Also, with power one demands respect. WE were naked to aggression, and fearful of exploitation, and we did not trust the persuasive advances of strangers. So what were we to do? Through great sacrifices, efforts, and determination, we got the power. Now we also demanded respect.

The foreigners saw us as an Asian country and therefore not deserving of respect. Compared to them we Japanese were classed as a third rate power, poorly equipped, and with untrained forces. Can one not see that this insult added to our anger? In later years, were we not within our rights to retaliate when we refused them any respect?

They embraced their humiliation and disrespect towards our people by setting up unfair stringent immigration laws, which was enacted by their governments to prevent us from migrating to their lands. Worse yet, they put in bias restrictive regulations and policies on those of us who already were living in their territorial jurisdictions. Their constant barrages of hate voiced by their politicians, people, and media, which

137

added to racial fears and jealousies, caused our people to suffer terrible mental and physical abuses.

They slandered us; they taunted us; they aggravated us; they called us degrading and insulting names; and even worse, they did all they could to try to molest and destroy our dignity. How much more can one tolerate all this without some kind of retaliation? How much longer can one restrain their accumulative anger from it turning to becoming hate?

We Japanese are a proud people with very sensitive feelings. We are recognized worldwide for our traditional mannerisms in the art of politeness. We generally are slow to anger, but pushed to the extreme limits, we can become dangerously explosive.

The demands by our Japanese people for retaliation caused our government and the Military to demand that our country act and become more aggressive, even if it means war. We were tired of being stepped upon. We were offended and furious with their propaganda, which constantly depicted us as the villains, whilst depicting the foreign invaders and exploiters as the poor victims.

Unfortunately, the unfavorable consequence of our wrath was, in most instances, the retaliation of our suffering caused by the foreigner's injustices. I guess the time has come for me to end this letter, which was typewritten by my good neighbor, Tanabe Ishida, who is a highly regarding and knowledgeable history teacher. He has graciously volunteered to assist me in my defensive informative letters and, time permitting, we will be able to send you more of these papers as soon as possible.

I also wish to include this part of a journal found in the Philippines, dated April 22, 1942, by an unknown soldier:

The amazing quick successes by our forces in the Philippines allowed General Tomoyuki Yamashita, Commander of all forces in Malaysia and Hong Kong, to take away one of the best battle-hardened divisions, the 48th from Lt. General Homma Commander in the attack on the Philippines, and had them shipped for the planned attack on Java, of the Dutch controlled East Indies, thirty days ahead of schedule. Lt. General Homma was given in replacement approximately seventy-five hundred mostly non-combatants from Formosa, the 65th Summer Brigade, which I served as an officer. We were excited and proud now to be in the heat of the war as this was an opportunity to give honor and victory to our Emperor and our country.

We were immediately sent into the Bataan Peninsula, in the Philippines, where the enemy were in full retreat and cornered. It was not long after we arrived that the enemy finally surrendered; that was in early 1942. We were told to expect approximately twenty-five thousand prisoners, but instead we were shocked to find we had over seventy-five thousand prisoners: twenty-five thousand Americans and over fifty thousand Filipino soldiers. We were unprepared to handle such a large mass. Our forces had no training in handling prisoners of war. The problem was so great that no one dared to tackle such an impossible solution.

Thousands of these prisoners were hit with malaria, dysentery, poison bites, jungle fever, cholera, diphtheria, starvation, and dehydration. Thousands more needed

140

urgent medical help for their war injuries. There was no water easily available and what water that could be obtained was nearly always contaminated.

The area was overgrown with jungles, wild animals, poisonous snakes, insects, and treacherous swamps. It is a very hot and humid country that without available drinking fluids you would die very quickly with dehydration.

Our military leaders were at a total loss as to how we could provide food, water, and medical assistance to such a vast amount of people, as we could hardly supply our own forces. We were aware that their survival would be grim. We had no alternative but to just proceed as if we knew what we were doing and hope for the best.

The next dilemma we had was how we move this mass of humanity. We were short of transports in this area as most the roads were nothing more than poor dirt paths. We finally commandeered approximately two hundred various transport trucks, which we planned to shuttle as many as we could to San Fernando where freight trains would then take them to Camp O'Donnell, a former

United States Army barracks near Clark Field Air Base. The rest of the prisoners unfortunately had to walk the approximately one hundred kilometers to get to the railhead.

No one realized the consequences of this mass movement. We had truck breakdowns and shortages of fuel, plus the aggravation of many flat tires due to the terrain. It was difficult for our officers to select soldiers as guards for the long march of prisoners to the railhead. Those appointed had to bear the sweltering unfriendly weather, the long distance march over terrible terrain, and had to hope that the diseases that were rampant in that area would not jeopardize their health. Many of these soldiers accumulative anger over all the past injustices done to our people by their countries desired some kind of retribution, while others had great difficult personal struggles in trying to restrain themselves. We are taught surrender is for cowards and traitors, and not deserving of any special treatment.

Well, we tried, but it really was a nightmare which was headed for disaster. Thus thousands of these prisoners escaped on their march into deadly jungles, and most of them eventually died. Thousands more suffered the same fate from diseases, war injuries, starvation, and dehydration, on their way to Camp O'Donnell.

Then again thousands died in similar fashion in our prison camps in the first few months, as we were incapable of providing for them.

At that time all war material, supportive supplies, equipment and men were in very short supply, and because we were on the offensive, our dire needs were a priority. Because we did not have, we could not give, but I believe that we did our best under these circumstances. We were victorious against the enemy but we lost the battle in the Bataan Peninsula against the diseases, especially malaria.

This area is the Philippines has more malarial mosquitoes per square mile than any other place in the world, and was a serious factor in causing much of our troop causalities. War is cruel and…

This is all that was found from this officer's journal as it was partially burnt. I hope this will help you honor our Japan. Ito, this is very important information that helps to substantiate the defense of Japan's honor. It also gives you some of the history in truth about the real tragedies that was inevitable in the battle of the Philippines. I sent his information to show you how thousands and thousands of the enemy had either suffered terribly, or died because of the tragedies of war.

The truth as related by this officer was that the area had been a nightmare, the responsibilities definitely impossible to cope with, and that death, unfortunately, became unavoidable. There is no doubt that a few of our countrymen were cruel and abusive to prisoners. Retribution is wrong, so let no country claim their innocence. I am extremely proud to announce that most of our forces on land, sea, and air abided by the Japanese Imperial military conduct code of honor. There is no doubt that 'war is cruel'.

Grandfather Soichiro

It was now late, and tired troubled Ito was finding all this information quite troubling. Sleep was his priority.

The next day Ito's mother gave him a large-sized official looking sealed brown envelope. The sender's name on the envelope showed that it was from Tanabe Ishida, who Ito immediately recognized as the highly qualified history teacher who lived next door to his grandfather. He eagerly tore open the envelope and inside he found a brief note attached to some pages, which Ito assumed was additional information on Japan's past history. The note read:

> I have decided to take it upon myself to send you added information as to the questions why we are the way we are, and try to explain what really happened to our Japan. Your grandfather and I have committed us to fight the many untruths written and spoken against our heroic Japanese people. We are determined to never let anyone destroy our national pride.

> I hope that the attached information will be of interest to you, especially if you decide to write your book about Japan's honor.

> Tanabe Ishida

> Fact: *Japan's prior move to take control of Korea*
> The king of that country, who was heavily influenced and

controlled by the Chinese, wanted the door shut to white foreigners. This caused the Western powers, including the United States of America, to covertly approve and encourage our country to go ahead and take all of Korea. This conniving move was accompanied by some very strong and stringent demands, including non-restrictive trade and port facilities for these countries. The Americans insisted that they also would be the sole distributor of all petroleum products, such as oil and kerosene, to all of Korea.

The British wanted special concessions in that they would have exclusive rights to all construction of most of the roads, bridges, and railways. This also included the construction of specific buildings in certain areas of Korea.

The French requested that they would be allowed to open Christian schools in Korea. Japan was to ensure their safety and also to allow the freedom for them to speak out on their religious beliefs.

All these demands and requests were granted to the Western countries by 1910 when Japan annexed Korea.

We Japanese did all the dirty work, while the Wester foreigners feasted on our efforts.

Fact: *The loss of indemnity from Russia to Japan in the war of 1904 – 1905*

The then president of the United States of American, Theodore Roosevelt, who had very little respect for Japan, brokered a peace treaty between the Russians and us. He was a belligerent person and he was opposed to any of our demands for financial indemnity against Russia. He felt that Japan was unfair in their demands and subsequently refused to include it in the peace treaty agreement.

We ask ourselves why? We firmly believe that what really occurred was the fact that the Western nations were directly and indirectly a close-knit monopoly by the association of their family relationships. Consider this; during the time of the Russo-Japanese war the following conditions existed:

- The Tsar of Russian, Nicolas II, married the granddaughter of the late English Queen Victoria;

- Wilhelm II, Emperor of Germany, had an English wife who was the daughter of the same Queen Victoria;
- Edward VII, King of England, whose father was from German royal ancestry, was also the son of Queen Victoria;
- They were all somewhat interrelated to each other.

Diplomats for these countries did not have much trouble in convincing the American Government to squash our indemnity demands, as the Americans themselves were just recently a British Colony and still had a strong affiliation to the British. This denial to us brought tremendous anger from all our people. This war with the Russians was very costly to us and we had a right to collect some kind of cash indemnity. This was the norm for centuries. Take the British for instance; they demanded a huge ridiculous sum in cash indemnities from China in the Opium War, which took over twenty years for the financial struggling Chinese Government.

It pushed us to become more aggressive and embed upon us a fierce determination to back it up with an awesome array of military muscle, which we eventually achieved at a terrible cost and hardship to our people.

<u>This was the first step to Pearl Harbour</u>

The Mukden, Manchuria Incident in 1931

Within only a short period of time, from approximately 1900 – 1932, the underdeveloped wastelands of Southern Manchuria were amazingly made productive with the electrified energy of Japanese entrepreneurs, traders, immigrants, and laborers. This was also made possible by our Government's enormous financial investments in the areas controlled by our forces.

Hundreds of thousands of Chinese, Koreans, White Russians (non-Communists), and many other different nationals, looking for a better life, flooded into these enclaves knowing that Japan's provisions and promises to provide good law and order assured safety for them.

Just prior to 1921, our secret agents had positive information that the then ruling Chinese Government leaders, who were supposedly being our friends, were planning to rid their country of all foreigners, especially the Japanese. They began to spread ugly rumors and hate about our people in Manchuria, and they also encouraged the Chinese people to boycott anything Japanese.

At that time of our history, our Japan and its people were in dire straits, suffering unbelievable hardships, poverty, unemployment, and starvation, caused by the worsening depression that affected the whole world. Our heroic military leaders had but one choice, and that was to annex the whole of Manchuria, regardless of the consequences and world opinion.

This we did, and in January 1932 we called it our state and named it Manchukuo. Our armed forces' efforts gave with their lives to protect our investments and interests, and to scream out at the foreigners for their uncaring and unfair restrictions on trade, which we depended on, with their protective tariffs and making us victims of economic warfare.

Can anyone imagine what would possibly have happened if we did not fight to take all of Manchuria? We felt convinced that our people, and all those foreigners living under the security of our armed forces in areas controlled by us, would possibly be in serious danger of being massacred by the Chinese. This would be similar to their attempted ruthless killings in the Boxer Rebellion of 1900 in Northern China by over two hundred thousand Chinese, which fortunately, because of our military efforts, they were not successful. This also would have encouraged the communist Russians to take all of Manchuria, which would have caused us serious concerns in regards to our other investments and interests, especially that of Korea.

In other words, if we did not move right away with the take-over of all of Manchuria, then we would be guilty of punishing our own people by the terrible consequences that inevitable would have followed. Whatever we did, whether right or wrong, was always done to give love and honor to our Emperor and all Japanese people.

Our war in China in 1937

We strongly believe that the 1937 war was started purposely by unknown parties. You are a foreign country enjoying the fruits of your exploitation and domination of the Chinese people on their territories. You naturally are in constant fear that at any time there could be a possible Chinese uprising similar to the one that had occurred in the Chinese Boxer Rebellion in 1900 against foreigners. So what could you do to slow down or temporarily hold back any unpredictable future organized actions against you by the Chinese?

You finally have an answer. Get the Chinese and Japanese, who were living side-by-side peacefully, involved again in another war against each other. Then the accumulative hate and concerns of the Chinese would be somewhat shifted away from you and concentrated instead onto the Japanese. The Japanese would find itself tied up in an undesirable war of attrition. With the weakening of these two Asian armed forces you could be assured of a continuance in the total control and dominance of certain territories that really belong to the Asian people. So you set up a plotted plan to set up a shooting incident involving both the Chinese and Japanese armed forces at a sensitive border area divided by the Marco Polo Bridge in China. It worked. War now breaks the peace between these two mighty forces.

Did the foreign country really set up this despicable plot? This we do not know for sure. A country or group of people who wanted monetary gain by the selling of arms to both side could have planned it. It could even be that the Chinese communist organizations who wanted to weaken the non-Communist Chinese Nationalists' armed forces with a prolonged war against us were the culprits, as that then they would be able to easily defeat the Nationalists in a war and declare China as a Communist State which would be backed by Soviet power and influence.

In 1937 we had the best-trained, best-equipped armed forces in all of Asia and the Far East. We also had one of the largest and most powerful navies in the world. Our military leaders issued standing orders to all our military personnel that they were to severely punish any enemy aggressors with savage retaliatory onslaughts. We wanted respect, and we expected respect. We were determined to never being pushed around by anyone anymore. This was nothing more than a clear warning to all aggressors that they would be contending with a very dangerous and powerful destructive force. We were confident of success until:

- The French shipped arms and supplies from Northern Indochina (Vietnam) to the Nationalist Chinese armed forces;
- The British did the same through the Burma Road, in Burma;
- The Americans were the most involved with their enormous unlimited financial assistance and huge caches of arms and supplied that they gave. And more was available if need be to the Chinese Nationalist armies;
- The Russians increased their assistance to the Communists Chinese from their borders in Northern China.

This was totally one-sided and unfair. It was humiliating and infuriating. It caused us much casualties and heavy financial material losses. We had many successes, but what was left was a terrible and costly road to a possible total victory for us. At this time our people's anger at these foreigners became volatile.

<u>This was the second step to Pearl Harbor</u>

Ito became very disturbed and depressed with what he had just read. He decided that it would be good for him if he could discuss his inner feelings with his parents. He headed for the sitting room where he found them reading the local news. They both acknowledged his presence with a slight glance and a smile. His response was to blurt out, "I want my grandfather back home again!" which broke the silence and their concentration, and appeared to captivate their full attention.

They abruptly and simultaneously responded, "We do too."

Pleased now that they were attentive to his emotions, Ito continued, "Grandfather's research work for the truth so far has been very impressive and full of surprises. I can only hope and pray that someday our Emperor and our people will bestow great honor to him, whose fact findings will be known and accepted world-wide."

Before he could speak any further, his mother, trying to relax, interrupted, "My dear Ito, I wish you would put to sleep any more conversation at this time as it is now becoming late."

Ito's father, disregarding his wife's plea, got out of his chair, put his reading glasses into his shirt pocket, and looked directly at his son, and said, "Yes, your mother is right, it is now late, but I have a few words that I would like to say that will only take me a few minutes. Your grandfather believes that whether we are young or old, whether we did right or wrong, we must accept the past, but only in truth. This then will give us peace of mind, integrity, and strengthen our national pride.

It is said 'a soul without knowledge is not good.' Therefore, let this be a message to all of us, who are Japanese, that we must never, never forget those who unselfishly gave their all for us.

So I feel that honor must be accorded, not just to your grandfather, but to all concerned, by our Emperor and Government in officially dedicating a special remembrance day each year for the bravery of all those who sacrificed, suffered, or died for our common good. If anyone tries to destroy our trade, enterprises, and interests, which may potentially cause our people to suffer starvation and poverty, if they provoke us and try to take our common liberty away, if they belittle us and show disrespect to our Emperor and people, then we have no clear choice but to vigorously counteract these actions even if it means serious military confrontations. We must always stand firm to protect our rights and the Japanese way of life on behalf of our Emperor and our people.

Finally, I like to say that shame and embarrassment will eventually drown those that were involved in the untruths made against us."

His wife, aware of her husband's speech, felt that this was too difficult and disturbing for her son to comprehend, interjected, "Please Subaru that is enough. Our Ito must move to get to bed."

"Just one more minute mother. I have something to say to father that is very important to me," Ito solemnly responded. As both his parents focused their attention on him, Ito continued, "It seems that the road to being proud of our heritage and our country was always available to each and every one of us, but sad to say there are some of us who have become deaf and blind to the agonized cries of our heroic soldiers and people on their voluntary efforts to give us a better life in the days gone by, including today and the future. Therefore, never again will I follow the road of misconceptions. I promise, with much apology to our Emperor, my family, and the Japanese people, that I will always proudly march behind the banner of our Rising Sun."

He paused, saluted, smiled politely, and headed for his room. In his room he found a big folder for him. Inside it he saw it was from his history teacher.

To Master Kobiyashi,

This is the final defensive research paper on Japan's honor. Your grandfather wants the two of us to prepare for the world to read and to honor the unbelievable bravery of our Imperial armed forces and that of our people in Japan's approximately one hundred year history.

You might now have committed yourself to wanting to write a book on Japan's honor, especially since you must have learned much from all the factual informative letters before you.

I want to strongly emphasize that our Imperial armed forces code of conduct and that of our people have never and will never condone atrocities. All we desire is that charges of brutality against us be not exaggerated or manipulated in order to satisfy the foreigner's propaganda.

The Capture of Nanking, China, by Japanese Forces on December 13, 1937

1. Charges made against our heroic Imperial armed forces:
   The needless deaths of approximately 220,000 to 350,000 Chinese people;
2. The needless total destruction of a city.

Facts:

1. Nanking, in 1937, had less than 250,000 residents;
2. Within two weeks after our capture of the city most normal services were provided or available to it residents. Therefore, the city was never totally destroyed.

Biased Propaganda:

With all the difficulties we had to face in trying to find the truth for our investigate research in regards to the Nanking incident, we have finally concluded that:

- Who witnessed these so-called tragedies? One foreign priest, one German diplomat, and less than twenty Chinese people. Not any one of them could provide proof of these absurd and damaging charges made against tour forces;

- Doctored photos were produced and shown to the world in order to shame our honor and people, as well as influence the exaggerated charges made;

- Most writers on the aftermath of the 1937 war in Nanking almost always credited their figures, of over 220,000 Chinese people killed, and strictly obtained from the first book written on the Nanking incident. In this way they were able to set themselves free from any condemnation of false or biased writings. Rather than spend honest time on truthful research, they preferred to use hearsay to write their non-fiction historical books. There tampered photos and hearsay information would never be allowed or accepted as evidence in any legitimate court of law.

It is not right to allow these books to be displayed in the non-fiction section of any library when in truth they should be set in the fiction section. Most non-fiction writers, mass media, eyewitnesses, and biased foreign propaganda, claimed that their figures of 220,000 to 350,000 were based on a population of 250,000 residents, plus an additional 750,000 Chinese refugees living in the city of Nanking at the time we captured it till the first week in February, 1938. Where do they get such ridiculous figures? In the first place, Chinese are an intelligent and wise people. Whenever they sensed that an attack was imminent on the city, that they were in, they would automatically flee for their safety to the vast wide-open spaces of the countryside with their families. They would also endeavor to try and take with them whatever possession they could wheel away or carry.

Now if the city were totally destroyed by our forces, as they have claimed, then it would be senseless for these same people who left to ever entertain the idea of wanting to come back so soon. So, therefore, there never were 1,000,000 people in that city.

Our military figures show less than 42,000 Chinese killed in our victory in Nanking. These figures are reasonably correct when we compare the death tolls of much more destructive attacks on other cities.

For instance:

		Approx. killed
Dresden, Germany	Almost totally destroyed in one large scale attack on February, 1945, by one of the largest armada of enemy bombers.	135,000
Tokyo, Japan	Wave after wave of heavy enemy bombers dropped tones of fire bombs	140,000

	(incendiaries) on 09/10 March 1945, which destroyed most of the city with the worst fire storm to ever hit a city in the history of the world.	
Hiroshima, Japan	An atomic bomb was dropped on August 06, 1945.	100,000
Nagasaki, Japan	An atomic bomb was dropped on August 09, 1945.	100,000

Even though these four cities were almost totally destroyed and devastated by tremendous destructive bombing raids they had way less death casualties than those figures claimed by some in the Nanking incident. To demoralize us and to get world opinion to censure us, the Western world and the United States of America, without any actual confirmed evidence, played a big role in the condemnation of our forces. They believed that the wide-spread news of the horrors that occurred in the city of Nanking might encourage the Chinese people to fight with more anger and resolve, as well as help them unite their political differences in the war against us.

<u>This was the third and final step to a forced Pearl Harbor</u>

Furthermore, on December 7th, each year, in special ceremonies, the Americans honor and mourn their dead who were killed by our Naval Air Forces in our forced attach on their Pacific Fleet which was berthed in Pearl Harbor, Hawaii, on December 7, 1941. There is absolutely nothing offensive to us Japanese with their yearly rituals, but what humiliates and angers us, by those supposedly good friends of ours, is that these ceremonies are always accentuated with derogatory disgust for us by their mass media, politicians, and their people. They shower the world with condemnation for our attack and derogatory remarks against our people.

I ask you, what reaction would the Americans have if we set December the 7th, each year, as a special day so that we could honor and mourn our heroic Japanese that died on that attack of Pearl Harbor? Or, instead, on that day we could have a great celebration all over Japan for our easy victory that day when we destroyed most of the Pacific Naval Fleet. I am certain that any of these actions would seriously affect the American-Japanese relationships. This would cause them to retaliate immediately in whatever way they could. How can you see the one-sided effect of their actions? Is this true friendship? Is this the way for good close friends to behave? Do they not realize that their actions are making us Japanese people into a more closely-knit-insulated society, and with it, a distaste and distrust towards foreigners?

History will show that we definitely did not, I repeat, did not, start the war. We were forced into a war. It is a simple equation for anyone to understand, no ships for the enemy meant no strangulating embargo for our people in Japan. We were pushed into a corner with no choices. Our country and people's welfare and security will always be our number one concern.

Now one can see why we did what we did at Pearl Harbor on December 7th. Let us look at what the British and American situations were on December 6th, 1941.

Britain was losing ground on their war with Germany and Italy. They suffered heavy losses in men and materials, including many of their Atlantic naval and maritime ships. Their empire of exploited territories in Malaysia, India, Burma, Hong Kong, And elsewhere in the Pacific, were protected by minimal poorly equipped forces, with a pathetic small number of naval warships. At this juncture of the war they were not in a position to do any better. Their main concern was the growing power of Japan who at any time could, if they so wished, invade or easily take over these poorly defended places. They also were afraid of possibly losing any or all of their territories and interests to local uprisings.

The then President of the United States of America, Franklin Roosevelt, and many of his top ranking military leaders, secretly desired to be involved in a war against Germany and Italy, but their hands were tied as they had to adhere to their Congress and to the majority of their people's wishes to stay out of other countries' wars, thus remaining neutral and an isolationist country. So now if they could somehow provoke the Japanese into some kind of military confrontation, then they might be able to convince their Congress and people that war actions by their forces were a needed necessity to protect American security and interests.

They believed that this would end American's isolationism, and after that it would be just a matter of time that they would be granted approval by their nation to declare war against Germany and Italy. So what did they do? Their conniving scheme was to threaten and belittle our Japan with an enforced embargo, and thus, aggravate us enough so that we would retaliate.

Our accumulative anger, as of December the 6th, 1941, was on the edge of being explosive, and they knew it. The British and Americans had broken our naval and diplomatic codes so that they were well aware that something was about to happen. They knew that a large Japanese naval force, with aircraft carriers, were prowling somewhere out at sea. The British were positive that we were going to attack the American Pacific Fleet in Hawaii.

The American President and his inner circles were convinced that if there were an attack it would be against the American in the Philippines. General MacArthur, the Commander of the Americans in that country, was constantly alerted to a possible attack by the Japanese, even as late as the 6th of December, 1941.

Now the British felt that the Japanese naval forces would not be successful in their attack on the ships berthed in Pearl Harbor, as the water there was too shallow for torpedo bombers and, should we attempt an attack, our forces would be no match against the might and power of this awesome Pacific Naval Fleet.

Why did they not warn the Americans? They were kept silent by the then Prime Minister of England, the late Winston Churchill, who wanted this attack to occur so as it might convince the Americans to break their isolationism and eventually somehow he hoped that American would come to the aid of the British Empire by declaring war against Germany and Italy.

On December 06, 1941, England was fighting for its survival. The British also felt that their silence could help in the destruction of Japan's naval power, and thus, diminish their ability in any future expansionist desires of Britain's poorly defended territories. The British knew that the Japanese where hurting terribly with the embargo and were desperately in need to supplant their country's needs. Now why did the American President and his inner circle of politicians and military leaders want war with Germany and Italy? We believe that on December 06, 1941, they were very concerned that the British and Russians were losing the war to these countries, and if they should surrender then it would seriously jeopardize American security. Also, another important dilemma is who would pay the huge outstanding debts owing to the United States of America for all the supply shipments made in sustaining the British and Russians in their wars in the last two years. So now you can see why I distrust foreigners; they are not truthful to each other.

After the successful attack on Pearl Harbor, the then president of the United States, speaking to the American people, decried foul and shame on Japan condemning us for the sneaky and cowardly attack without first declaring war. Did we really do anything unusual by our actions? See for yourself what history tells us. When you write your book, address this problem to the accusers, the Americans. Ask them to explain why, in 1846, did they, with their superior power, flagrantly and unjustifiably attack Mexico, whose majority population were mostly poor peasant farmers. The most important question is why they did this without any warning and without first declaring war. They will surely say that they had their reasons; and so did we. On top of their aggression, they illegally seized vast territorial sections of land from this poverty struggling nation, which today is a large part of their continental United States of America. Is this justice?

History has shown that the Americans were guilty of attacking without declaring war at least five times; the Russians seven times; the British thirty times; and the French thirty-six times. Many, many countries also have committed these same offenses. So I ask why do the Americans continuously condemn us every year on December the 7th This should never be.

They threatened embargo is we did not remove all our forces totally out of Indo-China and out of most areas in China. We said we would meet most of their demands, but only on the condition that all foreigners must also agree to remove all their forces totally out of Asian soil, including areas in the Far East. We then asked the Americans that, if they really believed in justice, freedom and equality for all men, as stated in their Constitution, then they must set an example to the world by returning all illegally seized lands to the Mexican and Hawaiian people. We also pleaded with them to release their stranglehold on Puerto Rico and the Philippines, and thus give these people back their dignity by letting them be totally free from any American prejudicial manipulations or interference, so that they alone could be in control of their own country and destiny.

Sad to say, we were rudely and totally ignored, including our requests. We can truthfully say that we tried, but did they? These demands were absolutely one-sided. The Americans knew that we would never accept them. Well. I hope this info will help you, and right now I believe we both have had enough of history.

Tanabe Ishida

Chapter 14

During one of their get-togethers, Grandfather decided he should speak to Ito about some aspects in regards to Japanese wartime bravery. This, he hoped, would in some way help to reduce some of Ito's pains.

Never at a loss for grandeur, and his military background, he tried to stand rigidly to attention, swaying somewhat, and then saluted his grandson playfully. With an expression of pride, he began to speak, "My dear Ito! When you write your book, I ask you please not to forget to describe the efforts, determinations, challenges, and dangers, that our heroic Japanese military forces, in its forced wars, constantly had to face. Our people must be informed how they pushed themselves to do their duty, always giving of themselves without complaint, so that we, the Japanese people, could have a better life. It is only right that every boy or girl, man or woman, whether they be young or old, should always remember those days in history, but also, always with pride."

Ito interrupted, "Grandfather, do not worry. My book will open the eyes of the world, and it will also bring grateful heart-warming tears from our people for a military that gave its all for us. We must never forget them."

"Well said, Ito," Grandfather interjected. "But if you let me, I would like to continue." Ito acknowledged that request with an affirmative nod.

"Good! Then let me speak. Visualize if you can, you are a Japanese soldier surrounded and overwhelmed by jungle. The day is hot, muggy, and humid. The sweat and humidity causes your clothes to stick to you. As a human you smell putrid. Your orders are to advance through that jungle. You walk with fear and caution, not of the enemy, but of swamps, poisonous snakes and insects, wild animals, and most of all, the dreaded malarial carrying mosquitos. You realize your options are bleak to zero. But do you give up or retreat? No! Never! Instead you push forward as best as you can to your destination. Night comes and you shiver from the cold. You carefully ration your water because most of the water available will be contaminated or undrinkable. You are constantly conscious of the fact that without water in the area that you are in that you would die quite quickly of dehydration. Your food might be no more than a handful of rice. You are a proud soldier, so you move on, embracing the 'Bushido Code' of the Samurais, thus giving glory to the Honorable Emperor, and to the Japanese people.

Maybe, instead of jungle, you find yourself in a desolate barren mountainous island. You patiently wait each day for an imminent invasion by the enemy. You scrounge for water, and constantly pray for rain. Your food, if available, is less than a handful of rice. Your hunger is constant. You try to sustain yourself by killing or capturing rodents or anything that moves, including insects. You learn to live, just as rats, in tunnels carved into the ground or mountains. You live dirty with filth and contaminated air. You, and if you have any family with you, have committed yourselves to fight or die in whatever way that is necessary for the common good of the great Empire of Japan. Your strength is reinforced by the fact that 'surrender' is not in the vocabulary of the heroic Japanese Imperial Forces.

Maybe you are fifteen years old. You tearfully write a heart-wrenching note to your mother telling her that you probably will never return home, as you are now headed for a secret training base where volunteers, if accepted, will be trained as Kamikaze pilots. You naturally include in your letter how much you love her and how much you will miss her. You try to explain to her the sanity of your determined actions and decision, emphasising that every Japanese, no matter how old they are, whether male or female, has an obligation to punish the enemy in whatever way they can, in retaliation for their wanton inhumane killing of our innocent women, children, and old men, with their senseless brutal bombing raids.

Because you are so young it does not take long for you to become homesick. You begin to be tearful, you feel so lonely and lost. On your way to your destination you come across the terrible devastation of the once great city of Tokyo. You are stunned and angry. The tremendous destruction, deaths, and casualties from four continuous days of fire bombings by the Americans finally shock your senses. You hysterically cry and cry for your Japan and its innocent people. You cannot believe what you see. You cannot believe that was purposely done by a freedom-loving country, the United States of America. You finally settle down, wipe your tears, and quickly move in to help the volunteers in that city. To you every Japanese life is sacred and therefore, your ambitions for revenge must sit on hold. In the few days that you helped changed your life forever, from youth to manhood."

His grandfather then stood up and asked Ito if this was too deep for him to understand. "No," he replied, "Please continue, this is very eye-opening and challenging to a writer."

His grandfather cleared his throat, and pointing his index finger at Ito, continued, "You could be a sailor or marine in His Majesty's Imperial naval forces. You are under the command of Soemu Toyoda, Combined Fleet Commander-In-Chief. You are told a small flotilla of ships, consisting of eight fast destroyers, one light cruiser, the Yahagi, and the giant Yamato, the largest and most powerful battleship in the world, will set sail on April 06, 1945, to do battle against overwhelming enemy forces in an effort to save Japan's embattled island of Okinawa.

On-route, on April 07, 1945, your small fleet is being attacked from the air. You notice that your destroyer that you are on suddenly is moving with extraordinary speed. Your ship then released a heavy smoke screen from its funnels in its attempt to protect the light cruiser and the battleship. You hope the attempt is not too late and successful. You are soon disappointed because to your surprise you observe from afar heavy smoke and explosive hits on the Yahagi and the Yamato. Worse yet, you hear more explosions and see flames and smoke close by from other Japanese escort destroyers. Soon you are informed that the destroyers Asashimo and Hsmakaze have now both been sunk.

Your ship gets calls for help in the picking up of survivors. But you, like all the other ships, are fully occupied in perilous occupational combat. The enemy continued to attack our ships with no letup. The Yahagi and its valiant crew fought off wave after wave of attacking aircraft. Unfortunately the overwhelming odds finally laid this streamlined light cruiser to rest. It sank with most of its crew still on board. Looking afar, we saw a continuous armada of planes, which never seemed to end, attacking the battleship Yamato. The fighting spirit and incredible firepower of this great ship made the enemy pay a high price in their air attacks, but sad to say, in the final throes, bomb hits after bomb hits eventually caused this giant of a battleship to explode into a tremendous huge fireball and sink with most of its heroic crew.

Two other destroyers, the Kasumi and the Isokaze were so badly damaged that our own forces purposely eventually scuttled them. The rest of them limped home extremely saddened but proud of Japanese bravery.

You must wonder why this flotilla had no vital air cover. Well, first of all these ships were manned mostly by volunteers. They knew that there was a shortage of fighter planes in their country and what was available was vitally needed to provide protective escorts for our Kamikaze pilots, whose heroic sacrifices have already caused the Americans to suffer heavy naval losses and casualties. We believed that their sacrificial actions would help to deter our enemies from any hasty invasions of our Japanese homelands.

Although Commander Soemu Toyoda's flotilla were naked to air attack, their spirits were clothed with the warm knowledge that their brave brothers would somehow at least have a chance to reach their objectives, thus giving them the opportunity to die gloriously for their love of the Emperor and all Japanese people."

Ito's grandfather then sat down, rested himself comfortably, and continued, "Somehow I am trying to tell you briefly certain scenarios of bravery which was only a fraction of what our people gave of themselves, for their love of our Emperor and for all our people."

Ito then interrupted, "Grandfather, this is all very educational, but what I cannot understand is why are we discussing Japan's bravery when certain serious charges made against Japan by foreigners have not yet been repudiated or challenged by you in your promise to defend Japan's honor?"

Surprised with this question Grandfather replied, "Such as what?"

Ito, looking at his notes, responded, "The foreigners' claim that we were guilty in trying to prolong the war, which had eventually and officially ended on September 2nd, 1945. They instead have proudly proclaimed to the world that their dropping of one atomic bomb on Hiroshima and one on Nagasaki were necessarily used to shorten the war by as much as six months to possibly a year. They believed that these actions helped save the Japanese homelands from further devastating destruction as well as prevented the deaths and casualties to thousands of people."

His grandfather, always one to speak with great pride and assertiveness for his country, replied forcibly but solemnly, "How could I ever forget to defend us from such damning charges. You must forgive this old man for being neglectful. So if I may, I would like to have the floor for just a few more minutes so as I can try to explain as simply as I can the truth of what historically really happened."

Ito knew he needed this vital defensive information for his book, so he nodded affirmatively for his grandfather to go ahead and speak.

His grandfather continued, "Well, it's like this! Our main adversaries were united in drafting a document which stipulated that there was only one way out for Japan, Italy, and Germany, to end their wars, and that had to be total 'unconditional surrender'. To us, at that time, the term 'unconditional' meant that the conquerors would have unrestricted and unlimited demands upon us. Also what was there to prevent them from any possible molestation or abuses of our people, especially our women? So what were we to do in our efforts to find a respectable and practical way to end our forced war actions with our adversaries? Our military and political leaders demanded that the word 'unconditional' must first be deleted before we would consider any of their demands to put a stop to these wars.

It is a positive fact that the present and past studies done, mostly by these same adversaries, have concluded that 'unconditional surrender', compared to just 'surrender', shamefully prolong wars.

Thus, on August 10, 1945, in our desire to save the wholesale slaughter of hundreds of thousands of our innocent women, children, and old men, from our enemies' further indiscriminate bombings of our cities, we made an appeal to our adversaries, indicating to them that we now were ready to put an end to our forced war actions. This we were willing to do only if our honorable Emperor's position as sovereign ruler of our people was maintained.

The next day we were extremely disappointed and saddened when they denied our request. This insulting response made us shelve our efforts for a solution to peace. So the war unfortunately continued, and with it, thousands and thousands of added casualties for all sides, as well as an increase by our foes in the inhumane devastating destruction of bombing of our civilian properties.

So I ask who really prolonged the war. They attacked civilians rather than military targets, backing this with their propaganda that in their future planned invasion of our islands they had serious concerns that there would be heavy casualties for them if they did not eliminate the defensive threat of the civilian population. To us, their actions on our innocent civilians were deplorable and unjustifiable.

They told the world, and also recorded this in their history books, that they were only concentrating their bombings on military targets, and these civilian deaths and casualties were unfortunate. This was not so. The facts prove otherwise. Our enemies knew that most of Japan's heroic Imperial forces of almost four million were on duty in the Pacific, or in Manchuria and China. They were also aware that only less than one million of these who were ill equipped were thinly spread out to defend the many islands of our homeland from any possible foreign invasions. Therefore, we must see through their untruths. Their attack on our innocent non-combative civilians of women, children, and old men, by their relentless bombings, was in reality an effort to win an easy victory. They believed that these indescribable actions would move our civilians to beg for mercy and thereby to demand our military and government to end all conflicts. So their fear was only for propaganda purposes."

He paused for a moment, and then trying to be sarcastic, continued, "Can you visualize the fear in their eyes when they are faced by our civilians who were fighting starvation and diseases, armed to the teeth with pitchforks, rakes, kitchen knives, umbrellas, rolling pins, and a huge arsenal of bricks from demolished bombed out buildings, yelling 'Banzai'."

This brought both of them to some laughter. Then he continued, "For some insane reason our enemies eventually decided to use nuclear bombs which had been fully tested developed, and available, in their attacks on our cities. It was also a way for them to learn more of this potential and dangerous new weapon's destructive power on the structures of a city with live human beings rather than just animals and dummies."

Remembering Kyoto and his two baby girls brought tears to his eyes. He did his best to control his emotions, wiped his eyes quickly and said, "You must excuse me, but my heart saddens when I speak on the tragedies caused by the atom bombs. Not only did they destroy a whole city with just one bomb, but also they killed and injured thousands and thousands of innocent people instantly. Also, there was different severity of blindness which came upon those that were near enough to accidently look at the high intensity light which was the result of the tremendous heat caused by the powerful explosion. Thousands of people that were situated in a certain radius of the bomb explosion suffered various types of burns from the heat of the explosion. Also, whole areas were now contaminated with the dangerous effects of the emission of nuclear radiation. As the days and months moved on, the death toll steadily increased into the thousands.

The two cities that were bombed are still not free from its past. They are faced with an abnormal increase of unexplainable deformed births and cancers, which many, including myself, are convinced were caused by the ever present staying power of the dangerous residues of nuclear contamination."

As he paused, Ito asked, "How do you personally feel about the insane and criminal attacks by the Americans on our two cities with their atomic bombs?"

His grandfather stretches out into a more comfortable position, took a deep breath, sighed, and replied, "The enemy at that time knew we were already considering an end to our forced wars. They did not need to use nuclear weapons as they had such tremendous air power which could flatten any one of our cities, at will."

Ito, with a sullen and concerned look, interrupted, "Then why did they?"

"Yes, why did they?" his grandfather replied. "Well, it's like this! The American Government and their military leaders wanted to placate their people, and at the same time trying to hide their incompetence in the Pearl Harbor fiasco of our successful forced attack on their powerful naval Pacific fleet on December 07, 1941, promised themselves that eventually some kind of retribution must be paid back to the Japanese Empire. This we all know they did on Hiroshima and Nagasaki.

We will always be imprinted by the nightmarish holocaust of these two cities, which was their retaliatory response. Unfortunately, the shame on our adversaries for their senseless revengeful actions on these cities will never be erased as they are now forever bound and recorded in most of the world's historical records. Furthermore, no other country in the history of the world has ever been attacked by such a gruesome weapon – except us. Most of the world's population, including myself, are totally against all nuclear weapons and its possible use by any country. Like I have said to you before, we may never forget but we must always strive in some way to forgive. We can and will accomplish much greatness by being a compassionate

people, always working towards a better world by opening our
hearts to friendliness, forgiveness, and understanding, for all,
especially in regards to our now very close friends, the people of
the United States of America, who have willingly and with care,
guaranteed our security. They also have become our number
one customer of imported Japanese goods. So there you are!"
his grandfather said with an air of pride, "I hope that I have
given you sufficient responsive information to your questions."

"Thank you grandfather," Ito answered approvingly. "You always
speak knowingly, and somehow you make our people proud to
be Japanese."

His father then interrupted, "Ito, before you go to bed we would
like to speak some words. I want to tell you that I am very proud
that you have shown your desires to write a book with such
convincing determination. If one is ambitious then one should be
prepared to face life's challenges with great effort. It is quite all
right for us to wish and strive for things that we do not have. But
we must always remember that it is improper for us to be
ungrateful or unappreciative of the things that we do have. Yes,
the road of life will surely have its many disappointments and
pitfalls, but if we are ever to become successful as a nation or
as individuals, then we try, try, and try again, to succeed. So,

186

with all that we have said, I hope that the eyes of your heart will in some way be influenced and strengthened by the words of wisdom."

Suddenly there was a total silence as he awaited a response from Ito. Feeling awkward, Ito moved slowly, glanced at his parents with appreciative grins, and with some shyness, replied, "Gee, thanks! Thanks for all your considerate concerns that have showered me again with so much of your love. I am so fortunate and thankful to be a member of this family."

Before he could continue his grandfather interrupted, "No, no, my Ito, we are the fortunate ones. You are our joy and the centre of our world, and we proudly look forward to you becoming one of Japan's greatest historical writers."

Chapter 15

One week later, just before school opening, Ito's grandfather got a brief urgent phone call from a very upset and tearful Setsuko, to the effect that Ito had been struck down by a vehicle and was taken directly to the Emergency ward at the local hospital with undisclosed head injuries. As fast as he could, he rushed to the hospital where he eventually found a hurting and distraught Sabaru and Setsuko cuddling each other as they sat in the waiting room of the Emergency ward. This stunning pathetic scene and the possibility of losing his grandson caused him to become very tearful as he cradled the both of them with his arms. As soon as he could settle himself down to speak he asked nervously, "How is he?"

A chocked-up Sabaru replied, "We do not know as yet. He was brought here straight from the accident." He paused to wipe his moist eyes, and then continued, "We were told to wait here, and as soon as they can they will provide us with the prognosis of his situation and injuries."

They sat there for some time in an eerie silence, each with their own thoughts, burdened with sorrow.

Suddenly grandfather Soichiro unintentionally blurted out aloud, "What has he ever done to deserve this?"

Before anyone could speak a doctor and nurse appeared seemingly from nowhere. This brought the three of them automatically to their feet. They held their breaths as they focused their full attention on these two strangers whose sullen faces, they felt, were a preliminary to dismal news. The doctor walked up to Sabaru and Setsuko and politely asked, "Are you Akihito Kobiyashi's parents?"

They both were so tense with suspense and depression that they found it hard, at that moment, to speak. Instead they nodded affirmatively. Not wanting to be ignored as an important member of this family, especially in such a dire situation, Soichiro proudly and loudly interjected, "And I am his grandfather!"

The doctor asked them all to be seated again. He then briefly explained what he had been informed of the accident and the actions the hospital had taken.

Pausing for a moment the doctor leaned forward, put his hands on Setsuko and Sabaru's shoulders, and looking at each one individually, said, "This is not easy for me to say, but as a doctor it is my duty to tell you that this unfortunate accident has put your son in a coma."

This information was a traumatic shock to the three of them. Setsuko broke down into uncontrollable sobs, crying out, "No! No! This cannot be. My little Ito!"

Although Sabaru and his father were deeply affected by Ito's injury, Setsuko's reaction moved them immediately to comfort and console her. Embracing his wife close to him, Sabaru spoke first, "Please, my wife," he said gently, "We all must somehow hold ourselves together and try to remain strong. We must remember that all things are in the hands of the Divine One, and maybe through our prayers can we hope that we might be granted the return of our son."

"Sabaru is right in what he says," Soichiro added. He then turned to the doctor and asked, "Can you please explain this coma?" Before the doctor could respond, Soichiro continued, "Even though I am old and have not many days, I ask for you to speak openly and honestly regardless if it's unkind to my heart."

"Doctor," Sabaru interjected sadly, "You may or may not be aware that our son has been treated for cancer and we were informed recently that his cancer is in remission."

"Yes, we know," the doctor responded with much compassion in his voice. A little concerned about Setsuko's possible uncontrollable reaction to all this, the doctor looked directly at her and asked in a caring way, "How about you? Can you handle any further discussion on this matter at this time?"

Trying to restrain her sobs, she replied almost inaudibly, "It is okay. We need to know."

The doctor then continued, "I will try to be as brief as I can. Coma is a deep state of unconsciousness. The patient feels no pain. There are never any guarantees on recoveries, but we are hopeful that Akihito is only in a state of reversible coma, which may be aided to recovery by the administration of large doses of barbiturates. Recovery proceeds by stages, each of which may vary in duration by several days, depending on the extent of brain damage."

He paused, stepped back so that he could glance at each one of them, bowed and said, "By the way, I am sorry that I have not introduced myself. I am Doctor Hiroshi Jimbo."

He then continued, "As a doctor, I am well aware that this tragedy is very hard on all of you, and also I usually find that this injury is difficult and puzzling for most people to understand. So as soon as we can, we will provide you with a well-detailed medical report on your son. In the meantime, you are now all permitted to see him for only a brief moment. We prefer that he be left alone for the first night, but tomorrow, and thereafter, family members will be allowed to sit by his bedside for as long a period of time as we deem is beneficial to his betterment."

They then were brought to his bedside. Tears ran down their cheeks as compassion tore into their hearts. All three felt devastated and helpless for this young man who looked so saintly with his eyes shut and peacefully asleep.

Setsuko immediately, but gently, moved to his beside. Even though his face was marred and bruised, to her she only saw a precious child of beauty. She ran her small hand ever so lightly and softly on his face, kissed him with a mother's most gentle caring touch, and while wiping her eyes, mumbled to herself a prayer. She then slowly moved back to the comforting and waiting arms of her husband.

Chapter 16

The next day was very tense and distressing for all of them as Ito unfortunately was till in a coma. Most times, if she could, Setsuko would hold onto one of his hands while sitting at his bedside. To make the day more pleasant mentally and, to medicate the pain in her heart, she would at times talk to him or sing him old traditional Japanese songs, convincing herself that Ito could hear even though his eyes were shut. She stayed and prayed often till it was time for her return home to look after her husband's needs. When she did get home she was pleased but surprised to find grandfather Soichiro who was in deep discussion with her husband in regards to Ito's unfortunate situation.

After the usual formalities she hurriedly headed to the kitchen to prepare the evening meal. Just before she could really get started the doorbell rang. She immediately stopped what she was doing and opened the door. To her surprise she saw a well-dressed man with suit and tie standing there holding a brown envelope in his hand. He greeted her with a bow and a courteous smile.

Before she could react or say anything he asked nervously, "Are you Mrs. Kobiyashi, Ito's mother?"

By this time both Sabaru and Soichiro were now at the door, "Yes, she is," retorted Sabaru, who felt uneasy with the presence of the stranger. "What is it you want, and who are you?"

The stranger again bowed and with an air of importance in his demeanor, answered, "You must be Ito's father?" Before Sabaru could respond the stranger continued, "My name is Toshio Nagasone. I am Ito's history teacher. I have brought you something important that belongs to your son."

Sabaru realized that their suspicions of this stranger caused them to forget their senses to every day Japanese politeness, so he immediately reached out and cradled his arms around the shoulders of this visitor, pleading for him to come in.

"No, thank you very much, it's very kind of you," replied Nagasone, "I just want to give you this, and explain to you what this is all about."

194

He then presented the envelope to Sabaru. There was total silence as the three of them looked at this stranger visit with mixed emotional feelings. He then continued, "Some time ago Ito asked me to help him write some letters to his mother, father, and grandfather. These were to be given to you if anything should happen to him."

"Please Mr. Nagasone, come in where it's more comfortable for all of us," Soichiro pleaded.

"Thank you, but I must leave soon, so please just let me finish. School will be closed for summer and in a few days my family and I will be away for a long holiday. I thought it would be wide and best for me to give these letters to you to keep, just in case. We are aware about the unfortunate accident to your son. We want you all to know that the Principal, teachers, and students wish and pray for Ito's recovery, and send their condolences to you."

Tears slowly moved down Setsuko's pretty face, and all the men were misty-eyed.

After he had left and they had thanked him, they headed to the sitting room unsure where all this really was about. Many questions raced through their minds. Their big problem and a serious one was what should they do with these letters.

After much discussions and indecision, they finally concluded that the right thing for them to do was to open and read its contents. They did. It was painful, tearful, and heart-wrenching to read, but its main content was 'LOVE'.

Here are the letters:

To my Grandfather:

Thank you Grandfather for being such a good friend. With your constant visits you have made us very close and also brought unbelievable joy and love to our lives.

You have awakened me to believe that all things are possible, and that no one has a right to try to take away anyone's self-esteem.

Yes Grandfather, I have much love for you, and I have the greatest admiration and honorable respect for you. Thank you for your patience, wisdom,

196

understanding, and determined efforts, in the opening up of my mind and eyes to the truth about our past history, especially in regards to the heroic Japanese people who suffered and gave their all for us in their 'forced wars'.

I want you to tell everyone that Ito Kobiyashi is proud to be Japanese. It is now time for us to restore national pride.

Thank you for your teachings in distinguishing between what is right or wrong, good or evil, truth or untruths. I want to thank you for believing in me and in honoring me with your encouragement and support to write a most important historic truthful book dedicated to Japan's honor.

I know that you will miss me and, I am sure that you will shed many tears for me, but I want you to remember that I am now free and at peace, without again having to face worldly trials.

I love you, and love you. I leave you with this, how many grandfathers can one get, just like you?

Your one and only loving grandson,

Ito

To my father:

As I am now older and wiser I can see the past much clearer. I know that it was not your fault that you had to be away, but love for you made mother and I sad. I missed you with a terrible loneliness, especially at bedtime. I cried many a night thinking how sad you must be being all alone away from us. I often wanted to just shout 'Father we love you and we want you to know that you are always close to our hearts'. Then reality would set in and to comfort myself I would silently pray for you.

Thank you father for your loyalty and love for us; you work so hard to provide for us, giving us such a comfortable life.

Thank you for your tenderness, guidance, and protective ways in your dealings with me. Thank you for all the thoughtful things you did to brighten up our days.

To me, dear father, you are the soul of this family, and mother the heartbeat.

I am sorry to disappoint you with my departure but I have no choice in the matter. I want you to know that you will forever feel the warmth from the glow of my love for you.

I am ever so grateful that I could be your son; my love for you has no measures.

Your son, Ito

Dear Mother:

How does one go about saying what is so precious to one's eyes. When I was young and afraid of the dark, or whenever I clamped my hands tight over my ears because I was scared of the sounds from thundering storms, you somehow always seemed to be there to comfort me, with your gentle caressing arms, and your assured responses, making me feel so safe, and by protecting me with your umbrella of love.

199

Whenever I am depressed or just hurting it's you, my mother, who makes every effort to go out of your way to bring sunshine to my eyes. But if I should cry you tried to wipe my tears with your emotional love. You are the wall of strength when I am weak, and no matter how I stumble, you always seem to be the one to pick me up. I wonder how many rivers of tears mothers of this world have shed. It is sad, but true, that if one could see the heart of most mothers, one would find it badly scarred by life's inner sorrows.

I want you to know how much I appreciate and love you, my dear mother. I have to be honest with you, I was fearful of my ill health at the beginning, but I want you to know, Mother, that as time went by, I learned and became fully aware of all the heroic efforts and sacrifices done for us in the past and present by our people, that I became ashamed to even consider my own life's problems, compared to what they put out and suffered for all of us.

What I also want you to know is that no matter what happens to me, I truthfully feel in my heart that I have been honored to be given so much love from our

200

countrymen, and from my ever-loving family. So Mother, please, no more tears that will dim your beautiful caring eyes as I can assure you that there will be no more dark clouds in the sky, only beautiful sunshine and peaceful serenity for me, forever.

My life now is in the hands of the Divine One who I assure you will take good care of me. Even if the door of life is closed behind me, I will always be able to feel you reaching out with your warm embraces. When you walk, you will feel me walking beside you. I love you my mother, and don't worry, I will forever be near you.

Some days you may grow weary in the struggles of it all, but please Mother, try not to despair as someday soon we shall all meet again. So please don't cry. I sincerely believe that this life, with all its great mysteries will surely someday come to an end, and we will all be together again with no more pains, sufferings and sorrows. We would be filled with joyous everlasting deep peace that the world shamefully was never able to give to any one of us.

Oh my mother, how I love you. You gave your love to me without limitations, which was always enhanced with your smiles, gentleness, and an understanding heart. Having a mother like you is in itself a lesson of love.

So thank you so much for being my mother. You are so special as well as honorable. I want you to know that I will be at peace and will be eagerly looking forward to the day we are a family again.

There is one more very important thing that I want you to know. Do you remember me buying a special gift to give to Tome, and then instead I later decided to give it to her older sister Henshe? Well, as you know, neither one got it, because I promised myself that it would only be given to someone special who would be the most important girl in my life. AS you know, sometime later I thought that Kimiko should receive this gift, as I believed, at that time, that I finally found my heart's first love, but something held me back.

Do you know why Mother? Well, it's like this. The gift that I still have belongs to none other than you, my dear mother, because you are my first love. I am extremely proud to have the privilege to be able to call you my mother. Thank you again and again for giving so much of yourself.

I love you ever so much – your son,

Ito

The End

If not Ito then who, in this wide world,

will write a book about Japan's honor?

Made in the USA
Charleston, SC
29 September 2015